THE OTHER SIDE OF
INNOVATION

THE OTHER SIDE OF
INNOVATION

SOLVING THE
EXECUTION CHALLENGE

VIJAY GOVINDARAJAN

CHRIS TRIMBLE

Tuck School of Business at Dartmouth

HARVARD BUSINESS REVIEW PRESS

Boston, Massachusetts

Library of Congress Cataloging-in-Publication Data

Govindarajan, Vijay.
  The other side of innovation : solving the execution challenge /
Vijay Govindarajan, Chris Trimble.
      p. cm.
  ISBN 978-1-4221-6696-3 (hardcover : alk. paper)
1. Technological innovations—Management. 2. Industrial management.
3. Strategic planning. I. Govindarajan, Vijay. II. Title.
  HD45.T744 2010
  658.4'063—dc22

                                                    2010006805

For Kirthi and Lisa

CONTENTS

Part II: Run a Disciplined Experiment

PREFACE

For the past ten years, we have been deeply immersed in the study of innovation within established organizations. We cannot think of a better topic to which we could have dedicated our energies. Through innovation, business organizations can change the world.

There is just one little problem. Business organizations are not built for innovation; they are built for efficiency. The day-to-day pressures are enormous, and combining a discipline of efficiency with a discipline of innovation is just damned hard.

One seasoned executive casually asked us not long ago, "Is innovation within an established organization even possible?" We do not regard the questioner as a cynic. We respect the question. In fact, here is a brutal truth: our organizations today are only modestly more prepared for the challenges of innovation than they were fifty years ago.

We are hardly alone in this view. Ray Stata, founder and chairman of Analog Devices, a $2 billion semiconductor manufacturer, is extremely thoughtful on the topic of innovation. About ten years ago, he said to us, "The limits to innovation in large organizations have nothing to do with creativity and nothing to do with technology. They have everything to do with management capability."[1]

The statement seemed provocative to us at the time. Today, after a decade of rigorous research, it seems an obvious truth. Most companies have plenty of creativity and plenty of technology. What they lack are the managerial skills to convert ideas into impact.

But how can this be? Today's global business leaders are smart and talented. Many are experienced innovators, veterans of the whiz-bang late 1990s when everyone seemed to have innovation on their minds 24/7. Most have collected a few hard-won lessons learned.

---

[1]Unless otherwise noted, quotations of business leaders come from interviews conducted between 2001 and 2010.

Nonetheless, there are limits to what executives can learn about innovation, even over an entire career. Innovations come in many shapes, sizes, and colors. They are context-specific. Experience from one endeavor often has little or no relevance for the next. A full perspective would require a career spanning multiple industries and multiple innovation types. Sadly, innovation initiatives are long and careers short.

Seeking insight outside their own experiences, executives often look to icons of innovation like Apple. Many have wondered: What is Apple's secret? What managerial magic led to the runaway success of the iPod?

But in ten years of research, not one of the companies we have studied has claimed to have innovation all or even mostly figured out. This is not a matter of modesty. In fact, these icons of innovation are usually trying to answer the same questions, only by looking in the mirror. They are asking themselves: What exactly did we do that made our past innovation efforts a success? How can we make innovation more routine?

This is what is currently happening, for example, at General Electric (GE). The company has a rich history of innovation successes, including breakthroughs in tungsten filaments for light bulbs, jet engines, and magnetic resonance imaging (MRI) devices for medical diagnostics. Nonetheless, GE faces the same difficulties we see everywhere and is now actively engaged in trying to figure out exactly what it has done when it has succeeded and how to reliably repeat it.

That is the current state of the practice of innovation, even in the world's best companies.

Nonetheless, we are highly optimistic. The organization of the future—the near future—will be much more adept at simultaneously delivering efficiency *and* innovation. (If you are eager to learn exactly how, please skip to the introduction.)

The Story of Management Research

We are so strongly optimistic because we have seen that while there are sharp limits to how much practitioners can advance knowledge about managing innovation on their own, partnerships between business and academia can be very powerful. And management research has only recently advanced to the point that a significant breakthrough is possible.

Believe it or not, until recently, scholars have not aggressively advanced the field of innovation. Given the number of business schools around the world engaged in management research, this is surprising to many. It is less so when put in historical context.

The story of ideas about management begins at roughly the start of the twentieth century, around the time that the first business schools were founded. Back then, management thinking was rooted in experiences in factories, railroads, and assembly lines. People and organizations were viewed as mere components in the machinery of production.

Progress in advancing knowledge about management was slow through the first half of the twentieth century, in part because business schools viewed themselves primarily as trade schools, not research institutions. By the middle of the century, however, leading thinkers had at least acknowledged that people are different from tools and that organizations are more like organisms than machines. (Physicists were advancing their field somewhat more rapidly. By then, they had developed the theory of relativity and cracked the secrets of the atom.)

In the latter half of the century, business schools expanded their charters. They dedicated themselves to advancing knowledge about management through rigorous academic research. Many business concepts that today seem basic and mainstream originated from this new commitment and, thus, are newer than many people realize. It wasn't until the 1970s, for example, that senior executives widely accepted that their number one job was a newfangled thing called *strategy*.

By the 1980s, there had emerged a single, dominant strategic idea: to sustain success, identify an attractive industry, carve out a strong position in it, and defend it however possible—by creating entry barriers, for example. The notion of *strategy as stability* was powerful. At the same time, it is hard to imagine a doctrine more antagonistic to innovation. The mantra of the 1980s was one of fierce resistance to change.

The 1990s brought a backlash. A new group of strategists insisted that playing defense was futile. Change is unstoppable, they argued. All competitive advantages inevitably decay. Companies that resist change, those that fail to innovate, soon die. Therefore, strategy cannot be about maintaining the status quo. It must be about creating the future. In other words, *strategy is innovation.*

This newer view of strategy is now widely accepted, and scholars are continuing to refine their ideas about the relationship between strategy and innovation. For example, there are many typologies that classify innovation efforts on the basis of their possible strategic impact. Innovations can be sustaining or disruptive. They can be radical or incremental. They can be competence-enhancing or competence-destroying.

While these classifications are useful in selecting *which* innovation initiative is likely to have the most powerful strategic impact, they offer little insight into *how* to make the innovations happen. Indeed, ideas about strategy and innovation have propagated much more rapidly than the managerial skills on which they depend. Can modern business organizations make *strategy as innovation* actually work?

Some of the most well-known researchers have taken a dim view of the possibility. Clayton Christensen has consistently warned that while established organizations will succeed with sustaining innovations, they will struggle mightily with disruptive ones. Chris Zook has recommended that companies take only small steps outside their existing business.

Their conclusions, however, are based on studies of what organizations have accomplished in the past, not what organizations might deliver in the future. Their research is akin to someone studying all the aircraft built through the mid-1940s, collecting voluminous statistical data, and claiming, on the basis of all available evidence, that traveling faster than the speed of sound is impossible.

Tell that to Chuck Yeager.

We believe that organizations *can* break the sound barrier. In fact, while acknowledging that there are still more questions than answers, we see no managerial reason why established organizations should be incapable of executing *any* innovation initiative.

How? The answers are becoming much clearer. There has been a dramatic and productive surge of research in the most recent decade. Our work is part of that surge. In this book, we offer practical new advice for senior executives, chief innovation officers, leaders of innovation initiatives, members of innovation teams, aspiring innovators, and all those who support innovation.

How We Produced This Book

The work that led to this book began in 2000, when we set our research mission: to learn by studying a variety of innovation endeavors in a variety of contexts, to generalize, and to prescribe. The endeavor has been satisfying, if lengthier and more labor intensive than either of us initially imagined.

Innovation research is challenging because very little can be quantified. Even a seemingly straightforward matter, such as calculating the profitability of a given innovation initiative, proves elusive. Corporations are under no obligation to make such information public. Furthermore, there are so many shared costs between innovation initiatives and other activities that five different accountants could easily provide five different answers.

The only effective way to study the management of innovation initiatives is to compile in-depth, multiyear case histories. Doing so is time consuming and expensive. It requires extensive interviewing, followed by the meticulous process of synthesizing hundreds of pages of interview transcripts and archived documents into meaningful narratives. This work requires access through unique partnerships with corporations, and corporations are generally willing to partner with only the top academic institutions.

We were fortunate to have the means and the opportunity to pursue this work through the William F. Achtmeyer Center for Global Leadership at the Tuck School of Business at Dartmouth. With the support of many, we have assembled dozens of multiyear case histories of innovation endeavors. We believe that ours is the most extensive library of innovation case studies in the world. Several of the case studies are summarized in this book.

Five years ago, at roughly the midpoint of our effort, we wrote *Ten Rules for Strategic Innovators—From Idea to Execution*. This first book was, in essence, a midterm report. Until then, we had confined our study of innovation to a special case—high-risk, high-growth potential new ventures, the most extreme form of innovation. Studying extremes is useful for researchers. Extremes reveal fundamental principles with great clarity.

That said, the most common feedback we received after publishing *Ten Rules* was, "How do I apply these principles to the initiative that I am involved with, which is not quite as dramatic as the case studies in *Ten Rules*?" At the time, we could make some conjectures. Now, we have answers. Our research is complete. We have collected case studies across the full spectrum of innovation initiatives—from small process improvements to high-risk new ventures. The principles and recommendations in this book span the full territory.

Our database includes one or more in-depth case histories from well-known and well-respected corporations such as Analog Devices, Cisco Systems, Corning Incorporated, Deere & Company, Dow Jones, Hasbro, Hewlett-Packard, IBM, Infosys, the New York Times Company, Stora Enso, the Thomson Corporation (now Thomson Reuters), and Unilever. (We have made these case studies available in full at www.theothersideofinno vation.com.) We also draw from interviews with several chief innovation officers and innovation leaders at companies including Aetna, Allstate, ABB, Ben & Jerry's, BMW, Cargill, Citibank, Electrolux, General Electric, Harley-Davidson, Kimberly-Clark, Lucent (now Alcatel-Lucent), Mattel, Procter & Gamble, Sony, Timberland, and WD-40, and reviews of publicly available materials about innovation efforts at companies including 3M, Amazon, Booz Allen Hamilton, Dell, Disney, DuPont, Eli Lilly, FedEx, General Motors, Intel, Johnson & Johnson, Kodak, Microsoft, Nucor, Oracle, Philips, Polaroid, Porsche, R.R. Donnelly, SAP, Seagate Technology, Southwest Airlines, Sun Microsystems, Toyota, Visa, and Walmart.

For ten years, this work has energized us. It has convinced us, beyond any doubt, that while the problem of innovation within established organizations is daunting, it is solvable. The reflexes of efficiency can indeed be augmented with the muscles of innovation.

Onward.

—Vijay Govindarajan
 Chris Trimble
 Tuck School of Business at Dartmouth
 Hanover, New Hampshire

Making Innovation Happen

THE CLIMBERS AWOKE just past midnight after hardly sleeping at all. They were excited and alert. They were among the nearly ten thousand climbers each year who attempt to reach the heavily glaciated summit of Mount Rainier in the northwestern United States. It is perhaps the world's most difficult climb that is accessible to novices, so long as they are accompanied by expert guides.

The first hour of the climb was easy. Each subsequent hour was harder. Finally, at dawn, the climbers got their first glimpse of the summit. It was as they had imagined—majestic and inspiring, gleaming in the morning sun. The climbers focused all of their energies on getting to the top.

With each step, however, their labors became more excruciating. Muscles ached. The air became thinner, and some of the climbers became dizzy. Some contemplated the very real possibility that they would not be able to make it. Each year, nearly half of those who attempt to reach the summit turn back unfulfilled.

But these climbers persevered. Step by step, they reached the summit. They were jubilant and exhilarated. Months of preparation had come to fruition. To be atop Mount Rainier is to sense that you are on top of the world. The city of Seattle lies more than fourteen thousand feet below.

But their adventure was hardly over. They still had to get back down.

Their expert guide was ever mindful, in fact, that the descent from Rainier's summit was actually the more difficult part of the expedition. Climbing a flight of stairs may be harder than descending. Hiking to the top of a local peak may be more difficult than the return trip. But Rainier is different. It is a dangerous mountain, one that claims a few lives each year.

The snow on the surface of the glacier can collapse into interior caves and tunnels, and climbers can slip into deep crevasses. As each hour passes, sunlight and rising temperatures soften the snow and increase the risk. Climbers are deeply fatigued and prone to mistakes.

No matter how many times they are told of the dangers in advance, climbers naturally relax at the summit. The glamorous part of the quest is over. The big aspiration—the big dream—has been fulfilled. The trip down is, instinctively, an afterthought.

Having invested very little of their emotional energies in the descent—and having little physical energy remaining—the climbers took their first steps down the other side of the mountain.

The Other Side of Innovation

There is a Rainier-like summit in the innovation journey. It is the moment a company says *yes*! That's a great idea! Let's take it to market! Let's make it happen!

Getting to the summit can be difficult. It might involve years of scientific research, months of building prototypes, endless creative brainstorming sessions, exhaustive market research, in-depth strategic analyses, intense financial modeling, and more. Dozens or even hundreds of possibilities might be eliminated before . . . finally . . . the search comes to fruition.

The challenge of reaching the summit lures many. It captures the imagination. The summit is majestic and inspiring. It gleams in the sunlight.

Indeed, getting a group of businesspeople engaged in a Big Idea Hunt is usually easy. Brainstorming sessions are fun! Out-of-the-box thinking is energizing! Ideation is cool! Not only that, generating a breakthrough idea is glamorous. It wins great status. If *you* come up with the brilliant idea, then *you* will always be associated with it.

Getting to the summit can seem like the fulfillment of a dream, but it is not enough. After the summit comes the other side of innovation—the challenges *beyond* the idea. *Execution*. Like Rainier, it is the other side of the adventure that is actually more difficult. It is the other side that holds hidden dangers. But because the summit itself has such strong appeal, the other side is usually an afterthought. It is humdrum. It is behind the scenes. It is dirty work.

Ideas Are Only Beginnings

Companies think far too little about the other side of innovation, and we are not the first to say so. In 2007, IBM ran an advertisement intended to convey that it could help its clients innovate. It featured a pudgy mock superhero sporting a capital "I" on his outfit who introduced himself as "Innovation Man." A bemused colleague asked, "And your job is?" The superhero responded with gusto, "*I* for Ideation! *I* for invigoration! *I* for incubation!" The onlooker replied, "What about *I* for *Implementation?*" Innovation Man answered, "I knew I forgot something."

We loved the ad. It captured so humorously and yet so perfectly the off-balance approach to innovation that is commonplace in corporations around the world. There is too much emphasis on ideas, not nearly enough emphasis on execution. Thomas Edison made essentially the same observation more than a century ago: "Genius is 1 percent inspiration and 99 percent perspiration."

Nobody listened.

Several companies have shared with us their maps of the innovation process. These maps are revealing. One typical diagram showed innovation as a four-stage process: *generating ideas, refining ideas, selecting ideas,* and, finally, like a lazy afterthought, *implementation.*

No wonder, then, that so many innovation initiatives hit a wall. The guiding managerial model for innovation is just too simple. It reduces to:

innovation = ideas

As a result, most corporations have more ideas than they can possibly move forward. Far too many promising ideas on paper never become anything more than . . . promising ideas on paper.

Here is an improved equation for innovation:

innovation = ideas + execution

Take just a moment to rate your company on a scale of one to ten, first for its ability to generate innovative ideas, then for its ability to execute them. Repeatedly, when we do this exercise with executives, they rate their companies relatively high for ideas—say, seven or eight—but quite low for execution—typically one or two.

Where is there greater room for improvement? Yet most companies, in their efforts to improve innovation, focus entirely on the Big Idea Hunt. Focusing on ideas may unleash more immediate energy, but focusing on execution is far more powerful. And innovation *execution* is what this book is all about.

A Tale of Two Recessions

When we launched the research that led to this book in 2000, innovation was all the rage. It was the height of the dot-com boom. How quickly things changed. By 2001, markets were in a tailspin and the diagnosis seemed clear. Too much innovation! Too much hype! Too much belief in the power of the Internet to transform the world overnight!

Yet, many of the visions incubated during the dot-com boom *did* come to fruition. It just took a lot longer than anyone anticipated. For example, it turned out that there was tremendous value in business-to-business e-commerce. It just turned out to be much more complicated than online retailing, and so it took much longer to get it right. And the Internet did turn the music and video industries upside down, but not until there was widespread availability of high-speed Internet connections. A better diagnosis of the dot-com bust is: "Great ideas, haphazardly executed." With a more careful approach to implementation, far fewer dollars would have been lost.

In 2010, as we completed our research, the economy was in an even deeper recession. But this time, innovation was not seen as the source of the problem. It was seen as the solution to the problem.

Can the U.S. auto industry reinvent itself? Not without a range of innovative new products. Can the health care industry find a way to deliver access and quality *and* keep costs under control? Not without commercializing entirely new approaches. Can the global energy industry create a future far less dependent on fossil fuels? Not without breakthrough victories in renewables.

There is no shortage of great ideas on how to address these major challenges. The critical questions, then, are: What did we learn from innovation failures of the past? Are we better prepared to convert great ideas into great impact? Are we ready for the other side of innovation?

Innovation Comes in Many Shapes and Sizes

Let's take just a moment to define *innovation* and, in doing so, define the terrain for this book. We take the broadest possible perspective. An innovation initiative is any project that is new to you and has an uncertain outcome.

People have often described their initiatives to us and asked, "Is that innovative?" The question always amuses us a bit. We've never really viewed ourselves as authorities on what counts as innovation and what does not.

We've found that there is very little value in trying to draw the line. From small and simple projects to grand and gutsy gambles, it is all innovation to us. When a salesperson experiments with a new pitch, it is innovation. When a company spends hundreds of millions of dollars to launch a high-risk new venture, that's also innovation.

That said, some innovation projects are much harder to execute than others. Sometimes the other side of innovation is a hop, skip, and a jump; other times it is a perilous descent from Rainier.

As part of our work, we've experimented with tools for assessing the managerial degree of difficulty of an innovation initiative. As it turns out, only two ratings are really needed: *routine* and *difficult*. There is not much middle ground. Well-managed corporations have mastered the other side of innovation for a subset of initiatives—the routine ones. This book delivers a prescription for all other initiatives—those that even the best-managed companies struggle with.

Before we do so, however, it is important to understand, briefly, what corporations have already mastered. What works? Why? And, more critically, what are the limitations? We look at two examples, Nucor and Deere & Company.

Continuous Improvement at Nucor Corporation

Nucor may not be a household name, but it is a remarkable company that unleashed the power of innovation in a decaying industry. Nucor makes steel. The company was of inconsequential size in 1970, but grew at an average of 17 percent per year to over $4 billion in revenues by 2000 while returning 20 percent on equity. During the same time frame, the

U.S. steel industry struggled as it wrangled with competition from abroad, threats from alternative materials, and strained labor relations. In fact, the industry delivered one of the worst profitability and growth records in the economy.

Nucor's success cannot be attributed to a breathtaking strategy. Its strategy was plain and simple: operate efficiently and compete on costs. Therefore, Nucor could succeed only by innovating every day.

The company's model for innovation was not mysterious. Nucor galvanized the energy and ingenuity of its workforce. The company did so with two essential policies:

- To stimulate *ideas,* Nucor cross-trained its employees and rotated them among plants.

- To *motivate* each employee to find innovative ways for improving production efficiencies, Nucor paid for results. Base salaries were actually low for the industry, but bonuses ranged from 80 percent to 150 percent of base wage. Those bonuses were paid weekly based on the number of tons of steel produced that met quality standards.

Thus, Nucor's model for innovation can be reduced to a simple equation:

innovation = ideas + motivation

This combination created an environment in which innovation happened through grass-roots action, as close to the front lines as possible. When employees saw a way to improve performance, they simply took the initiative to make it happen.

We have seen several well-managed companies make the *innovation = ideas + motivation* model work. In fact, when companies speak of a "culture of innovation," this seems to be what they mean—an environment in which creative ideas are plentiful and employees are empowered and motivated to do something with them.

However, as powerful as this approach can be, and as potent as it proved for Nucor, consider what this model for innovation is *not* capable of. It quickly runs into a brick wall. What if pursuit of a particular innovation initiative requires more than the small sliver of free time that individual employees have left over after fulfilling their day-to-day responsibilities?

Imagine that you work on the factory floor at Nucor and you have a big idea for improvement; maybe it is a major reconfiguration of materials flow through the steel mill. Even if it is a powerful idea, it is far beyond your ability to pursue while on the job. You might try to gather some friends to contribute their energies, but even if you are very persuasive, the total resources available to you are tiny—a handful of employees and their spare time. Any project requiring more resources than that withers. It can get little further than the idea stage.

Innovation in the form of continuous process improvement is certainly possible with an *innovation = ideas + motivation* model. And, as Nucor's experience shows, thousands of small steps can add up to a powerful result. Still, larger innovation initiatives require a different approach.

Product Development at Deere & Company

One of Deere & Company's most important product lines is world-class tractors for large-scale agriculture. These are complex machines. Hundreds of people are involved in designing and bringing each to market. It takes about four years and $100 million to design just one.

A company as well managed as Deere doesn't spend $100 million casually. It brings as much discipline to the task as possible. In fact, the company treats product development much like any other business process. It tries to make it efficient and reliable.

Indeed, over many years, Deere & Company has gone to great lengths to perfect its recipe for developing new tractors. Documentation of the process constitutes, literally, several weeks of reading. As a result, everyone on the product development team understands his or her role. Everyone understands that he or she is accountable for completing each step in the design process on time and on budget.

Deere & Company's capability to quickly and efficiently launch new tractors with cutting-edge technology is impressive. At a high level, its approach to innovation is shared by many companies. It can be reduced to a simple equation:

innovation = ideas + process

The execution challenge is reduced to creating a step-by-step process that can be used again and again. Such an approach can be powerful.

However, any formulaic process for innovation is also a narrow and specialized capability. It relies on each new product being mostly similar to previous-generation products. Make design changes that are too significant (we will zero in on "too significant" in chapter 1), and any well-oiled innovation process stumbles. A more robust model for execution becomes necessary.

Getting Beyond the Limits

The *innovation = ideas + motivation* formula can generate thousands of small initiatives, but does not support projects requiring resources beyond a few people and their spare time. The *innovation = ideas + process* model can efficiently crank out innovation after innovation, as long as each initiative is mostly a repeat of prior efforts.

Well-managed companies are adept at both models for innovation execution. We will give them no more attention in this book. We focus only on innovation initiatives that lie beyond these capabilities.

In a fast-changing world, innovation beyond the limits of these two models is critical. But what are the alternative models?

Here is a story that is familiar to us from our research and is probably familiar to you as well. It is a composite of the innovation struggle at many of the companies we have studied.

Times are getting tougher for the CEO. Growth in core markets is declining. Customers are demanding more. Competition is intensifying. Margins are shrinking. To restore high performance, the CEO announces a major effort to stimulate innovation and organic growth. After a few months of generating ideas, researching ideas, refining ideas, analyzing ideas, reviewing ideas, contemplating ideas, comparing ideas, testing ideas, and turning ideas into business plans, the CEO makes a commitment to the single best option, the "Great Idea."

What's next? The road gets considerably steeper. First of all, *who* will move the idea forward? Everyone in the company already has a full-time job. In fact, the company's best leaders have the most critical jobs sustaining excellence in the existing business. Nonetheless, the CEO recognizes just how important the initiative is and taps a fast-rising, ambitious, up-and-comer. The CEO tells the leader that he has a great deal of latitude. Just do what is necessary, he says. Break some eggs if you have to.

The young leader is excited about the opportunity. He views it as a powerful chance to differentiate himself from his peers and advance his career. Furthermore, he is thrilled by the open-ended charter. It is all so empowering! Just make it happen! It seems like a dream job.

It is not. The aspiring leader has been set up to fail. He just doesn't recognize it yet. The first few months go well, but reality soon sets in. It is not easy for one person to create change in a large corporation. After one year, the leader feels as though he is trying to make innovation happen inside an organization that is, in every way, determined to fight his every move. The general manager of the company's largest product line is anxious about the possibility that the innovation will cannibalize him. Marketing is uncooperative, worried about possible damage to the company's brand if the new product fails. Manufacturing is upset that it has to schedule small, inefficient runs for the new product. Salespeople are reluctant to push a product without a track record. Human resources is unwilling to waive compensation rules to hire a few experts that the project badly needs. Finance is concerned about margin dilution. Information technology claims that the project is too small to warrant exceptions to standard systems and processes.

Undaunted, our hero summons all the energy, courage, and moxie he can. He pushes, and then he pushes harder. But the path doesn't get any easier. In frustration, he goes a step further, fashioning himself a rebel and a subversive. He fearlessly, or maybe even recklessly, flaunts authority. He tells himself daily that it is always easier to ask forgiveness than it is to ask permission. *Break all of the rules* becomes his mantra.

In the end, however, it is our leader who is broken, and the innovation lost. Sadly, it is only in fantasies and fairy tales that heroic rebels overcome long odds to achieve glory. In the real world, they fail, and their company fails with them.

Our hero is not at fault. The company's simplistic model for innovation is to blame. It is a model that puts the full burden of execution on an individual leader:

innovation = ideas + leaders

This model is commonplace. After committing to a Great Idea, many companies put great emphasis on finding the Great Leader to execute it, as though that is all that is required. The assumption is that a talented and empowered leader ought to be able to overcome whatever barriers an entrenched organization erects.

The notion is convenient and attractive. In fact, just a couple of decades ago, most of the formal research on the other side of innovation focused on the personal leadership traits and characteristics of innovation leaders. And one of the most frequent questions we get when speaking to executives is, "How can I identify the best innovation leaders in my company?"

We do not dismiss the importance of innovation leaders, but we believe it is dramatically overemphasized. Choosing a talented leader is never enough. One person against "the system" is an extraordinarily bad bet.

Organizations Evolve for Performance

But why is it such a bad bet? Why is it that innovation leaders so often feel that their biggest enemy is not the competition but their own company? There is a simple answer. *Organizations are not designed for innovation.* Quite the contrary, they are designed for ongoing operations.

Companies do not start out this way. At launch, there aren't any ongoing operations. Everything is innovation. But this quickly changes. Soon after a start-up reaches its first commercial success, a new challenge emerges—making operations as profitable as possible. Demands for profitability only get stronger as the company grows and matures. This evolution is natural and unavoidable. Early investors want innovation, excitement, and growth. Later investors want profits. They want reliable profits.

To satisfy investors, companies strive for productivity and efficiency, and their organizations evolve to deliver it. They focus on serving their customers better than their rivals. They excel at being on time, on budget, and on spec. They get a little bit better, a little bit faster, and a little bit cheaper, every day, every month, and every year. They are disciplined and accountable at every level.

The pressure for reliable profits, each and every quarter, is *the* force that shapes and molds companies as they grow and mature. Inevitably, organizations evolve into what we call *Performance Engines*.

Fundamental Incompatibilities

Strong and healthy companies have strong and healthy Performance Engines. At the same time, the stronger the Performance Engine gets, the more difficult innovation becomes. The first rule of innovation is simple: *Innovation and ongoing operations are always and inevitably in conflict.*

The most readily apparent conflict is the tension between short-term and long-term priorities. Every company struggles with it. Under pressure to deliver profits every day, the Performance Engine instinctively swats down innovation initiatives—or any project, for that matter, that cannot make an immediate contribution. Managers at middle and low levels who face rigid performance targets each quarter can be powerless to overcome this reflex.

But the incessant drive for immediate profits only partially explains the struggle to innovate. At more senior levels, executives routinely overcome short-term pressures and allocate capital to projects with long time horizons.

Thus, there must be deeper forces at work. As it turns out, the most powerful conflicts between innovation and ongoing operations are easily overlooked. They are subtle. They lie in the *method* of the Performance Engine. The method is the same, in every company and in every industry. To maximize results, the Performance Engine strives to make every task, every process, and every activity as *repeatable* and *predictable* as possible.

It is hard to understate the power of repeatable and predictable. The more repeatable a business process, the more amenable it is to being broken down into ever-finer subtasks. Specialization of labor has been acknowledged as a powerful expedient to efficiency since the birth of the industrial age more than two centuries ago. Predictability is just as powerful. When past performance can serve as a baseline for future expectations, each individual in an organization can be held accountable for meeting clear and proven standards of performance.

The techniques for managing Performance Engines through the relentless pursuit of repeatability and predictability are well understood. They have been honed and refined for many decades. In fact, the very language of business is the language of Performance Engines. Consider how businesses keep score. Accountants, as a first premise, consider businesses to be ongoing concerns. This year's activities will be more or less a repeat of last year's, and last year's performance is the best predictor of this year's performance.

Repeatability and predictability work. Modern corporations have mastered the process of building and perfecting Performance Engines. In doing so, they have delivered tremendous gains in efficiency and thus tremendous gains in living standards worldwide.

At the same time, the greatest strength of a Performance Engine—its drive for repeatability and predictability—also establishes its greatest limitations. By definition, innovation is neither repeatable nor predictable. It is exactly the opposite—nonroutine and uncertain. These are the fundamental incompatibilities between innovation and ongoing operations. They strike right at the heart of how leaders are trained, how organizations are designed, and how performance is measured. They make it impossible for the Performance Engine to tackle innovation initiatives outside of continuous process improvements (which are small enough to fit within the slivers of slack time that are always present, even in the most efficient Performance Engines) and repeatable product development efforts (which can follow Performance Engine–like processes).

Break All of the Rules?

The fundamental incompatibilities are daunting. No wonder, then, that innovation leaders so frequently view the Performance Engine as their primary antagonist. No wonder, then, that innovation leaders so frequently believe that you must break all of the rules to succeed. No wonder, then, that so many innovation leaders see themselves as entangled in a heroic long-odds battle against a bureaucratic octopus.

But the break-all-of-the-rules mantra, while understandable and widely shared, is poison. There are at least three reasons.

First, innovation leaders *need* the Performance Engine. Most obviously, it is profits from the Performance Engine that *pay* for innovation. Treat the Performance Engine as your enemy, and you may soon find yourself without funding. In addition, innovation plans almost always call for leveraging one or more assets or capabilities that are managed by the Performance Engine, such as a brand or a sales force.

Second, to managers responsible for ongoing operations, "break all of the rules" sounds a lot like "break the Performance Engine." Innovation leaders, take note: antagonizing the Performance Engine is a *really bad idea*. When leaders responsible for the Performance Engine sense danger, they fight. And, because the Performance Engine is bigger and more firmly established, it almost always wins. In the process, innovation dies.

Finally, "break all of the rules" sounds an awful lot like "no rules." Indeed, innovation leaders often sound as though they think they deserve to be free to pursue their dreams, as in, "We, the Innovators, are a blessed and superior lot. We are, and should be, exempt from your bureaucratic rules and your plebian demands for day-to-day efficiency and accountability." This, of course, fuels the antagonism. In addition, the attitude is meritless for innovators. Though innovation must be evaluated differently, there is no reason that innovators cannot be every bit as disciplined and accountable as the Performance Engine.

The break-all-of-the-rules mind-set is most appealing to the youngest innovation leaders. They are the ones most likely to view the Performance Engine as a mindless bureaucratic machine that deserves no respect, while casting themselves as the superheroes who can defeat the vast forces arrayed against them by fighting head on. This is nothing more than youthful fantasy at work. It is not a practical approach to making innovation happen.

Mutual Respect

Instead of fighting the Performance Engine, the innovation leader must build a partnership with it. There must be a relationship of mutual respect.

Respect comes more naturally when innovators recognize that an innovation initiative, even a major one, is just an experiment. Innovation may very well signify the future, but the Performance Engine is the proven foundation, and if it crumbles, there is no future.

Also, innovators develop a healthier relationship with the Performance Engine when they recognize that they are not up against some sort of evil anti-change faction. Conflict with the Performance Engine is not rooted in laziness, timidity, complacency, convention, or conservatism.

Quite the contrary, conflict with the Performance Engine derives from the endeavors of good people doing good work. It arises from efforts to achieve the most basic goals of every business—producing, delivering, selling, marketing, servicing, and more—every hour of every day, with speed and efficiency. This may sound routine. But is it? Modern global corporations perform juggling acts that are just short of miraculous. They smoothly and gracefully coordinate operations scattered across multiple continents. Like a Porsche racing down the autobahn, the Performance Engine is awesome.

Indeed, innovation leaders must honor the Performance Engine. They must be committed to helping the Performance Engine sustain its excellence just as they are committed to their own projects. And, in formulating the recommendations in this book, we have taken, as our first obligation, that we must do no harm to the Performance Engine's existing capabilities.

However, a bit of humility on the part of the Performance Engine is also important. Despite their daunting capabilities, Performance Engines are not all powerful, and they are not immortal. The range of innovations that they can tackle is woefully insufficient. Companies that operate strictly within the bounds of Performance Engine capabilities fail to evolve. Eventually, they die.

Just as innovators need the Performance Engine, the Performance Engine needs innovators. It is a relationship of mutual dependency, one that demands mutual respect.

The Distinct but Disciplined Approach

While "break all of the rules" is toxic as a leadership mantra, there is some truth in the notion. There *are* different rules for innovation.

In fact, one of the most common reasons that established companies struggle to execute innovation initiatives is that they fail to appreciate just how differently they must treat them. The group working on an innovation initiative cannot *just* be a home to a more creative culture. It cannot *only* be a collection of people who like to think outside the box. These are helpful attributes, but they are insufficient. There must also be deep change. Many of the fundamental principles for managing an innovation initiative bear little resemblance to the fundamental principles for managing the Performance Engine: *The innovation team must be* distinct *from the Performance Engine.*

Critically, however, *distinct* does not mean *undisciplined.* Companies often err when they assume that innovation cannot be managed because there is too much chaos, serendipity, and unpredictability.

While it is true that innovation initiatives are *unpredictable,* especially in the earliest stages, this does not make them *unmanageable.* All too often, innovation leaders use uncertainty as an excuse to avoid accountability. But innovation should not be about freedom or rebellion or escape from the exacting demands of the Performance Engine. The innovation team must be just as disciplined as the Performance Engine. Companies must adopt a distinct but disciplined approach to innovation.

Addressing the Fundamental Incompatibilities

To get from a foundational philosophy of distinct but disciplined to the next level of practicality, we must return to the fundamental incompatibilities.

- Because ongoing operations are *repeatable,* while innovation is *nonroutine,* innovation leaders must think very differently about *organizing.*

- Because ongoing operations are *predictable,* while innovation is *uncertain,* innovation leaders must think very differently about *planning.*

Alas, most companies think carefully about neither organizing nor planning when launching an innovation initiative. All too often, companies jump straight from "Great idea!" to "Go make it happen!" In doing so, they implicitly assume that the way that the Performance Engine organizes and plans can work for innovation too. This is an excruciatingly poor assumption.

In some contexts, businesspeople tend to think quite carefully about organizing and planning. When thinking through a company's overall logic, most managers think at three levels. At the top level lie mission and strategy, in the middle sits organizational design, and at the tactical level are policies and processes for execution. This is Business School 101.

Nonetheless, when most managers think about innovation, they overlook the middle level entirely. (See figure I-1.) An improved model for innovation *must* include organizing and planning:

innovation = idea + leader + team + plan

Indeed, *innovation = idea + leader* is really just half of a model. Because of the dominance of this half-model, most companies vastly overproduce ideas and do better than necessary at selecting leaders. But they struggle

FIGURE I-1

Innovation's missing link

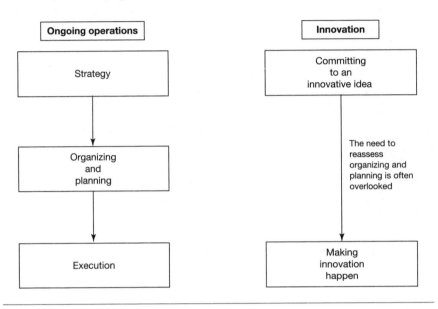

mightily with organizing and planning. Without careful and distinct models for each, most innovation initiatives are dead from day one. The fundamental prescription in this book is that every innovation initiative needs a special kind of team and plan. Specifically: *Each innovation initiative requires a team with a custom organizational model and a plan that is revised only through a rigorous learning process.*

Note the emphasis on *each* innovation initiative. Until the concluding chapter in this book, we focus on how to execute a *single* innovation initiative. Businesspeople frequently jump quickly from thinking about one to thinking about many. Instead of asking, "How do I make this very important initiative a success?" they ask, "How do I make innovation happen throughout my organization?" But you must learn to walk before you learn to run.

A Team with a Custom Organizational Model

Building a team with a custom organizational model is a significant and difficult undertaking. Companies rarely make the perfect choices the first time. From fear of failure or for lack of familiarity with any organizational model other than that of the Performance Engine, they often shy away from the task.

Even when they rise to the occasion, companies typically underestimate the degree of difficulty of the challenge. By now, most executives have heard a tidbit of conventional wisdom—that many innovation efforts require some kind of separate organization. The advice is accurate but vague. A separate organization that does what exactly? Separate how? Does separate mean isolated? Independent? Even worse, the advice gives the impression that there is a simple black-and-white, yes-or-no decision to be made.

But much more than a simple separate-or-not-separate decision is involved. The right team usually combines both dedicated assets and Performance Engine assets. And there are many further considerations. Sometimes, building the right team requires hiring and empowering a new group of experts. Sometimes it requires discarding existing titles and job descriptions. Sometimes it requires commissioning a special senior executive council to mediate the conflicts between innovation and ongoing operations.

When senior executives and innovation leaders meet to discuss how to organize an innovation initiative, they should start by committing to take no shortcuts of convenience. To give in to whatever is quick and easy when building the team is to be weak. It is to be *un*disciplined.

In the core of this book, we will explain the principles for building the right team with the right custom organizational model for any innovation initiative. We will address such questions as:

- Besides the leader, who should be on the team? Should they come from inside or outside the company?

- Does everyone involved in the innovation initiative need to work on it full time? Can some sustain their existing responsibilities?

- How should the team be organized? How does this differ from "normal" for the company?

- What specific conflicts between the innovation initiative and ongoing operations are likely to arise? How can they be anticipated and resolved?

- To whom should the team report? What are the supervising executive's most important responsibilities?

A Plan Revised Only Through
a Rigorous Learning Process

Just as with organizing, companies typically underestimate the magnitude of changes that are necessary when planning an innovation initiative. The way you plan an experiment is much different from the way you plan a proven operation.

Performance Engine plans are loaded with data. While it is true that even the most mature businesses face uncertainty, far more is known than unknown. Expectations can be grounded in history; the past is a reasonable guide to the future. Managers are expected to deliver results equal to or better than what has already been proven possible.

Innovation plans, by contrast, are loaded with assumptions. Sure, some hard facts are available, but more is unknown than known. The past is no longer precedent. Thus, the innovator's job cannot be to deliver a proven result; it must be to discover what is possible, that is, to learn, by converting assumptions into knowledge as quickly and inexpensively as possible.

Some innovation projects will disappoint. That is inevitable. What is unforgivable, however, is to draw the wrong conclusions and fail to learn from the disappointment.

Innovators learn when the work of creating and revising plans is guided by a rigorous learning process. To support such a process, each innovation initiative should have a separate, dedicated, stand-alone plan. Because experiments are so different from ongoing operations, it is crucial to separate results prior to analyzing and interpreting them.

When launching an innovation initiative, senior executives and innovation leaders should also commit to interpreting results from innovation projects accurately and dispassionately. This is easy to say but devilishly difficult to do. Interpreting results from experiments is more complex than analyzing proven operations. Sources of bias are numerous and hard to avoid. And, the well-honed planning practices of the Performance Engine can easily get in the way.

In the core of this book, we explain the essential principles for following a rigorous learning process. We address such questions as:

- What should the planning process for the innovation initiative look like?

- In what ways should the planning process for the innovation initiative be connected to the planning process for the rest of the company?

- How can progress be assessed? By what metrics and standards? When can the company's existing metrics be applied?

- How should we evaluate the innovation leader? How is this different from "normal" for our company? What accountabilities are appropriate?

A Heavy-Duty Solution

In the back of your head, you may be thinking, "This all sounds good, but wait a minute. In our company, we innovate every day, but we don't take these kinds of steps. A special team with a custom organizational model? A separate plan revised through a rigorous learning process? That must be complicated and expensive. We'd bring innovation to a halt if we tried to do that for every initiative."

We have no doubt that your organization is innovative, even if you have never contemplated such steps. Remember, some forms of innovation are well within reach for the Performance Engine, including continuous process improvements and product development initiatives that are similar to past efforts.

Performance Engines may not be able to tackle every innovation initiative, but they are incredibly powerful. In addition to being masters of efficiency, reliability, and quality, they are also capable of delivering growth, and sometimes explosive growth, by expanding geographically, by targeting growing segments, by capturing market share from weaker rivals, and by making acquisitions.

Still, Performance Engines' nonstop quest for repeatability and predictability takes many innovation initiatives out of reach. Each such initiative requires a special kind of team and plan. There is simply no alternative. Is it a heavy-duty solution? Yes. Is it necessary? Absolutely.

The specific notion of chartering a special team for an innovation initiative is sometimes resisted because it is in conflict with at least two common assumptions about organizations and innovation. First, there is a widely held assumption that the ideal organization is one that is perfectly aligned. On the surface, this makes a lot of sense. It simply means that everyone is pulling in the same direction. But note that a special team with a custom organizational model is clearly a deliberate step away from perfect alignment. Nonetheless, taking this step is both normal and necessary. Striving too hard for perfect alignment kills innovation.

Second, we often hear leaders talk about their desire to embed innovation in the very fabric of their organizations, so that innovation is happening everywhere, all of the time. This sounds powerful too, but it is a flawed notion. The conflicts between innovation and ongoing operations are steep. You can't possibly embed one inside the other.

On one hand, more complex innovation initiatives and ongoing operations *can* coexist in the same *company*. This book, in fact, is all about how to make the unlikely combination work. But they cannot possibly coexist *throughout* a company. There must be some purposeful separation of the two and then careful management of the interactions between them.

How to Read This Book

Our fundamental prescription is that each innovation initiative needs a special kind of team and a special kind of plan. Part I of this book focuses on the team and part II focuses on the plan. The two parts of the book are conceptually independent of one another and can be read in either order. We start with the team only because it is the more intuitive of the two.

Both parts I and II include a brief but important introduction followed by three chapters. The chapters should be read sequentially. In part I, each chapter builds directly on the previous one. In part II, the first chapter gives a complete overview of our prescription, and the subsequent chapters take closer looks at particularly challenging dimensions of it.

The sequence of chapters does *not* follow a time line for executing an innovation initiative. We hope that you will digest the full book and then keep it as a ready reference. On any given day, you may find principles from almost any part of the book to be relevant.

There are numerous examples of specific initiatives at specific companies throughout. We use these illustrations for a variety of purposes. For example, we open each chapter with a brief example that makes a simple point, one that sets the stage for the chapter. We also occasionally use very short anecdotes in the body of chapters to add some color and to reinforce an important point.

Most chapters also have a few examples that are intended to highlight some of the chapter's key recommendations at a more granular level. In some cases, we've provided more such examples than is strictly necessary in order to hit as close to home as possible for a variety of readers, industries, and innovation types.

A constellation of executives and managers must come together to tackle the innovation challenge. Each can benefit from this book in different ways.

For some audiences, we recommend close study of every chapter.

Innovation leaders. This book is aimed most squarely at leaders of innovation initiatives. When we address *you* from this point forward in the book, we are speaking to the innovation leader.

We assume that you are the junior-most leader whose responsibilities span not just one aspect of the initiative, but the overall project. You are responsible for building the team and making it effective, despite the fact that in most cases you will not have complete control. Not everyone involved will report solely to you. Some people on the team will also maintain Performance Engine responsibilities, so you will have to partner with Performance Engine leaders.

We also assume that you own the plan for the initiative more than any other person. You are the single point of accountability. The plan includes all activities required to execute the initiative, whether you control them directly or manage them through internal partners. It is the vehicle through which the initiative's progress is assessed and through which your performance is evaluated.

Members of the team. The best-prepared team members fully understand the challenges their leaders face. In addition, they must consider: What legacies of my experience working within this organization (or other organizations) might I need to leave behind to be successful on this project? What performance metrics might no longer apply? How might I have to adjust my expectations of my peers?

More-senior audiences will want to read chapters 1 through 6 with a focus on the most essential differences between innovation and ongoing operations. They will find the conclusion to be of particular interest.

Supervisors. The innovation leader will report to someone who we will call the *supervising executive*. While we frame our recommendations in chapters 1 through 6 in a language that fits the innovation leader's perspective, our recommendations frequently extend beyond what the innovation leader can control directly. In outlining what innovation leaders need and should reasonably expect from their organizations, we are implicitly coaching the supervising executive to meet those needs. We offer direct advice to supervising executives in the conclusion.

By the way, we have deliberately chosen the term *supervising executive* instead of the more commonly used term *sponsor*. We dislike sponsor because it makes the job sound easy or even trivial. A sponsor just provides occasional support. But the supervising executive has a critical job. Few innovation initiatives succeed without a deeply engaged one.

CEOs and chief innovation officers. To reach their highest aspirations, CEOs and chief innovation officers must scale up from single innovation projects to routine innovation successes. They must *institutionalize* innovation. This is a high aspiration, but the journey is much shorter once the core principles for managing *single* innovation projects have been mastered.

Thus, in the conclusion, we offer a few guidelines for managing *families* of similar innovation initiatives. Also, in the conclusion, we offer a teachable point of view on innovation that CEOs and chief innovation officers can share with their entire organizations.

Some audiences will find particular interest in certain chapters.

Performance Engine leaders who also support an innovation initiative. Chapter 3, which focuses on conflicts between innovation and ongoing operations, is a crucial read for this audience.

Human resource professionals. To appreciate the magnitude of departures from organizational norms that are often necessary for an innovation initiative to succeed, human resource professionals will want to study in particular chapters 1, 2, and 3.

Finance professionals. To understand how to differentiate their approach to interpreting innovation results from their approach to interpreting results of ongoing operations, finance professionals who influence the evaluation of innovation projects will want to study in particular chapters 4, 5, and 6.

Making Innovation Happen:
Observations and Recommendations

1. The real innovation challenge lies beyond the idea. It lies in a long, hard journey—from imagination to impact.

2. The Performance Engine is powerful and capable. It delivers productivity and efficiency, it is capable of growth, and it has *some* ability to innovate. It can tackle continuous process improvements and product development initiatives that are similar to past efforts.

3. Beyond these limits, fundamental incompatibilities between innovation and ongoing operations make it impossible for the Performance Engine to innovate on its own.

4. Because of the incompatibilities, innovation leaders often imagine themselves as rebels fighting the establishment. But one person against the bureaucratic octopus is an extraordinarily bad bet.

5. This book's fundamental prescription: *Each innovation initiative requires a team with a custom organizational model and a plan that is revised only through a rigorous learning process.*

6. Despite the inevitable tensions, innovation leaders must strive for a relationship of mutual respect with the Performance Engine.

PART I

Build the Team

J UST AS THERE IS A WIDE VARIETY of innovation initiatives, there is a wide variety of teams that push them forward. However, all these teams have something in common. They are all internal *partnerships.*

The two entities in the partnership are the Performance Engine and a Dedicated Team. We will refer to the subset of Performance Engine personnel who are directly involved in executing the innovation initiative as the Shared Staff. Therefore:

project team = Dedicated Team + Shared Staff

To be completely clear with our terminology:

- The term *project team* refers to the partnership.

- The Dedicated Team is, as the name suggests, dedicated to the innovation initiative *full time.*

- The Shared Staff is part of the Performance Engine. It executes or supports a portion of the innovation initiative *part time.* Simultaneously, it sustains excellence in ongoing operations.

The partnership is tricky because the Dedicated Team and the Shared Staff are, of necessity, quite different from one another. The Dedicated Team is custom-built for the project, and it has a new and unfamiliar organizational model. The Shared Staff's organizational model, by contrast, already exists and does not change.

The combined organizational model, depicted in figure 1-1A, is very flexible. Any division of responsibility is possible. In some cases, the Dedicated Team will execute nearly all, say, 90 percent, of the initiative. But a fifty-fifty split or a ten-ninety split is also possible. It depends on the nature of the innovation initiative and the capabilities of the Performance Engine.

FIGURE 1-1A

Organizing an innovation initiative

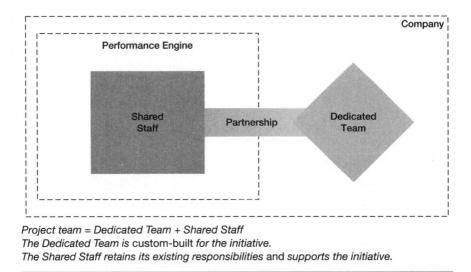

Project team = Dedicated Team + Shared Staff
The Dedicated Team is custom-built for the initiative.
The Shared Staff retains its existing responsibilities and supports the initiative.

The big-picture steps for building the project team are intuitive:

1. *Divide the labor.* Decide how responsibilities for executing the initiative will be split between the Dedicated Team and the Shared Staff.

2. *Assemble the Dedicated Team.* Determine who will serve on the Dedicated Team and how to define their roles and responsibilities.

3. *Manage the partnership.* Establish clear expectations for each partner and mediate the inevitable conflicts that will arise between the two.

We will explore these three steps in the next three chapters.

CHAPTER ONE

Divide the Labor

A T SUPERCOMPUTING 2004, IBM announced that it had built the
world's fastest computer, dubbed Blue Gene. The design was revolutionary because Blue Gene was not powered by the world's most powerful
microprocessors. Instead, it was powered by a massive network of rather
ordinary computer chips. As such, the design effort was different from any
prior IBM product development effort. Rather than relying on the Performance Engine, IBM created a Dedicated Team to get the job done.

In late 2005, Deere & Company won a gold medal at a prestigious
industry conference for its about-to-be-launched tractor for large-scale
agriculture. The 8030 tractor was cutting edge, a best-in-class technological marvel. Over four years in development, the 8030 was an innovation
that Deere & Company took great pride in. Yet, Deere did *not* build a Dedicated Team for the job. It was tackled, in its entirety, by Deere's Performance Engine.

The Performance Engine Has Limitations

When launching an innovation initiative, step one is to decide what parts
of the project you need a Dedicated Team for and what can be left to the
Shared Staff. To make the right choice, you must accurately assess the
capabilities of the Performance Engine. The choice is crucial. In some
cases, as with IBM, a Dedicated Team is needed for much of the job. In
other cases, as at Deere, one is not needed at all.

Because building a Dedicated Team takes time, energy, and money, it is
tempting to ignore the need for one. There is great excitement at launch.

Thinking about how to organize a Dedicated Team can seem like a distraction. Indeed, it is rarely as much fun as working on the innovation itself.

Therefore, the natural preference is to give as much of the task as possible, even the entire initiative, to the Performance Engine. Unfortunately it is very easy to overestimate what the Performance Engine is capable of. Rare is the company that assigns too little to it. We have only seen situations in which companies ask too much of it. And in speaking with executives about innovation, we almost never come across one who is eager to admit that a particular innovation challenge is beyond the capabilities of the existing organization. Their pride is understandable. They see impressive capabilities. They have a "can do" spirit. Nobody likes to say "no, we can't," and in most contexts, this is a positive trait.

Remember, however, that whatever role the Performance Engine takes on, it must simultaneously sustain excellence in ongoing operations. To do so, the Performance Engine must sustain its insatiable drive for efficiency. Inevitably, as the Performance Engine becomes more efficient, it also becomes more specialized, and its flexibility in supporting innovation diminishes.

It is a mistake to ask the Performance Engine to operate outside the confines of its specialty. The limits are rigid. Simply asking everyone involved to think differently or behave differently will not work. If you ask the Performance Engine to tackle a task that is outside its limits, it will either fail at the task or succeed only by disrupting existing operations.

Neither outcome is acceptable. Building a Dedicated Team is preferable, despite the extra effort required and even though it may appear to cost more because a Dedicated Team may require a formal budget approval, while a part-time effort from the Performance Engine may have no explicit cost.

Understanding the Limitations

The Performance Engine faces two limitations. The first is intuitive. To take on a task, the *individuals* within the Performance Engine must have the necessary skills.

That rule is much easier to state than to follow. It is natural to overestimate the capabilities of people you know when the alternative is taking a risk hiring someone you don't know. A simple question to check yourself: if you were building a new company from scratch to pursue the innovation initiative, would you make it a priority to lure people away from your current company? If the answer is yes, then your Performance Engine passes the first test. It has the necessary skills at the individual level.

The Performance Engine may not pass the second limitation, however, which is far more constraining and far more frequently overlooked. In fact, the most common reason that companies overestimate the capabilities of the Performance Engine is an instinctive but flawed logic that equates the capabilities of the Performance Engine with the sum of the capabilities of the individuals within it. It is easy to see immense individual talents and conclude that the organization as a whole can achieve almost anything.

But the limitations of the Performance Engine are a function both of the skills of the individuals *and the work relationships between them.* What person A and person B can accomplish together is not just a function of A's skills and B's skills; it is also a function of how A and B are accustomed to working together.

As a result, the capabilities of the Performance Engine are always *much narrower* than the aggregate total of the capabilities of the individuals inside. Those individuals have been tied together, that is, their efforts have been *organized* for a very specific purpose.

Work relationships evolve to meet the needs of the Performance Engine. They adapt to achieve efficiency through specialization of labor and through repetition. The work relationships in the Performance Engine are defined, in part, through formal understandings and arrangements about who is responsible for what and who has power and authority. But they also evolve informally. After you work with someone for a while, you develop many implicit agreements about how you work together.

Once in place, the work relationship between a pair of individuals is very difficult to change. Even under the best circumstances—removing the pair from their Performance Engine roles and responsibilities—it takes a conscious, explicit, and determined effort to do so. There will be substantial inertia. The pair will naturally continue to relate to each other in the way that they always have, even if the work challenge in front of them has changed dramatically.

But we are not talking about the best circumstances; we are talking about what the Performance Engine can handle even while it sustains excellence in ongoing operations. Changing work relationships under these conditions is impossible. The demands of ongoing operations are constant and pressing and act not to change but to reinforce the existing relationships. As long as A and B remain under Performance Engine pressures, there is no chance that their work relationship will change. Therefore, if the work relationships inside the Performance Engine are inconsistent with what is needed for a certain portion of the innovation initiative, then that portion *must* be assigned to the Dedicated Team.

This is the rule that should guide the division of responsibilities between the Dedicated Team and the Shared Staff for *any* innovation effort, whether it is a new process, new product, or entirely new business; whether the innovation is incremental or radical; whether it is disruptive or sustaining. But how do you assess whether Performance Engine work relationships are consistent with the demands of the innovation initiative?

Work relationships have three essential dimensions—depth, power balance, and operating rhythm. In the remainder of this chapter, we will define these dimensions and describe their significance using several examples. We start with several illustrations that show the limits of the Performance Engine within the product development function. We chose these examples because they are particularly vivid. The same rules apply in every function, however, as we will show toward the end of the chapter.

Limitations of Deere & Company's Product Development Organization

Product development teams are often considered the centers for innovation within a company. As such, it is natural to assign existing product development groups heavy responsibilities in executing innovation initiatives.

But be careful. Product development teams are like any other part of the Performance Engine. They have limitations that are tied to the nature of the work relationships within them.

Deere & Company's product development group, the one that built the award-winning 8030 tractor for large-scale industrial farming, provides a fitting illustration. The group excelled at Performance Engine innovation. Over a period of about fifteen years and four design iterations (the 8030 was preceded by three models, the 8000, 8010, and 8020, launched at roughly four-year intervals), the group mastered the *innovation = ideas + process* approach.

Deere did not start from scratch with each design. Each was an improvement over the previous design, incorporating new features and technologies without fundamentally redesigning the tractor. Nonetheless, in each iteration, the stakes were high. The 8030 was the most capital-intensive product development effort in Deere's history. And Deere faced a tough constraint. The time line for 8030's launch was fixed. Due to tightening regulations for diesel emissions, Deere would not be able to sell the 8020 tractor after January 1, 2006.

Therefore, developing the 8030 was a job that *had* to be on time, on budget, and on spec. In short, it was a job for a Performance Engine, and Deere's product development team was a Performance Engine in every sense. The group documented the design process in great detail to make the process more repeatable. It also gathered extensive data during each design effort so that the process was predictable. The leadership team set specific time and budget expectations for each step in the process.

The group was disciplined and accountable, and it delivered. Deere launched ahead of the January 1, 2006, regulatory change. Customers responded enthusiastically. They particularly welcomed the 8030's remarkable fuel efficiency at a time of rising oil prices.

Deere's product development capability is valuable. Nonetheless, in its effort to stay atop this market, Deere also takes on numerous innovation challenges that are *beyond* the capabilities of this particular product development team. Thus, the company is constantly confronted with decisions about when to work within its well-oiled product development process and when to work outside it.

To understand Deere's product development organization—to understand what it *can* and *cannot* do—some background is necessary.

The Modern Industrial Tractor

Modern machines have made agriculture incredibly efficient, freeing millions from the labors of the field. "Tractor" may not mean much more to you than "big lawn mower." If so, you'd find it eye opening to actually ride the 8030, a $300,000 machine when fully loaded.

You'd probably be surprised, for example, when you found yourself looking skyward just to glimpse the top of the rear tire, nearly seven feet off the ground. Once up the ladder and inside the enormous enclosed cab, you might be just as surprised by the ubiquity of electronics, including computer screens. And, once in motion, you might be caught off guard by the comfort of the ride. An independent electrohydraulic suspension eliminates 90 percent of the vehicle's vertical motion as it passes over bumps, ruts, and rocks.

You would also find the turning radius impressively tight for such a large vehicle, an engineering feat accomplished by building a special drop-box transmission that enables the engine to be mounted high and the wheels to maneuver underneath. But, really, did you expect to have to steer? Full-time steering is a dated notion. Not only do the 8030's onboard computers plot the most efficient route to cover every inch of field, they handle most of the steering too.

The tractor is the workhorse of farming. Yet, for all its technological sophistication, it does little on its own. It tows or pushes farm implements for all crops and all seasons—tillers, planters, sprayers, cutters, scrapers, harvesters, and more.

Farm Economics

While there are still many individuals who farm as a hobby and as a lifestyle, large-scale farming is a business. The tractor, at the center of the action, is a major capital investment. The economics of farming are closely tied to the economics of owning and operating a tractor. For farmers facing the tough realities of unpredictable weather and volatile commodity prices, tractors are one of the few economic drivers that farmers can actually exert some control over.

To run the farm as efficiently as possible, farmers seek fuel-efficient and powerful engines that can tow large implements. To minimize the total distance the tractor travels, they appreciate precise routing and steering. So that drivers can work from sunrise to sunset with few breaks, they like a tractor with a comfortable ride.

Still, ask farmers what they want from their tractor more than anything else, and the answer is quick and consistent. It is *reliability*—perhaps followed quickly by how fast it can be fixed if it breaks. The cost that farmers are most concerned with, by far, is the cost of an unexpected breakdown, especially during the short and unforgiving weather window for harvest.

Deere's Product Development Organization

Like any Performance Engine, Deere's product development organization evolved for efficiency through specialization of labor. Few individuals were experts on the tractor as a whole. Most had in-depth expertise in just one component. Each person's efforts were dependent on, and had to be coordinated with, the work of others.

A small and newly formed product development organization might take an ad hoc approach to coordination. One that aspired to maximize efficiency, however, would, with experience, hardwire the coordination task in job descriptions, schedules, formal process steps, and so forth.

That's what happened over time at Deere. Each of thousands of work steps was scripted. The relationships between component-level experts were formally defined. In fact, there were several managers dedicated full time to further specifying and improving the process. Work relationships also evolved informally, as pairs of individuals gained experience working together.

The network of work relationships within Deere's product development organization can be further described on the three critical dimensions of depth, power balance, and operating rhythm.

DEPTH. Some pairs of individuals in the organization had very deep work relationships, while others hardly knew each other. For example, pairs of individuals *within* a component specialty tended to work very closely together, while connections *across* specialties tended to be weaker.

Some cross-specialty connections were much stronger than others though. As it turns out, wherever there was a mechanical, electrical, or spatial connection between components in a tractor, there was a work relationship between specialists in the product development organization. For example, the engine designers had formal relationships and routine interactions with the drivetrain designers. They depended on one another.

Thus, the organization mirrored the product. Where there were connections in one, there were connections in the other.

POWER BALANCE. The power balance in work relationships was heavily shaped by customer priorities. Specialists who were instrumental in delivering on a critical customer need were more powerful than those who did not.

For example, because Deere's customers cared so deeply about reliability, there was a heavy complement of quality and reliability experts, and they were influential. They ensured that every engineer instinctively worried about reliability problems, and they created an extensive process for reliability testing including over fifteen hundred specific verification and validation steps.

OPERATING RHYTHM. Developing a tractor for large-scale agriculture is a complex, multiyear endeavor. Thus, the product development team adopted operating practices and habits that were consistent with this large-scale and long-term reality. For example, while engineers *within* specialties collaborated daily, coordination *across* component specialties was only necessary at longer intervals.

Interactions between the product development team and the rest of the company were also tuned to a long-term rhythm. For example, the general managers running the large-tractor business would not receive feedback from the market (sales figures, comments from customers) for nearly five years after the initiation of the design process. Ties to the corporation's human resource planning and capital budgeting processes also reinforced the multiyear operating rhythm.

Locating the Limits

For the 8030 effort, the network of work relationships within the product development organization was a strength. Change the product being developed, however, and strengths become weaknesses. Take the Performance Engine out of its sweet spot—that is, outside of the narrow bounds of its specialty—and a Dedicated Team is required. Consider the following three examples, which show how the depth, power balance, and operating rhythm of existing work relationships each create a limitation.

DEPTH. What if Deere wanted to pursue a major design revision? If the new project altered design at the system level—that is, it modified the way that the components within the tractor were linked together—then the component-level experts would have to work together in new ways. They would have to develop new work relationships that mirrored the new component connections in the new design. Deere would need a Dedicated

Team to tackle that portion of the effort that had unfamiliar connections between components.

POWER BALANCE. What if Deere wanted to design a product with a new value proposition? Examine any strong product development organization and you'll find that the balance of power between individuals mirrors the customers' priorities. When a company wants to develop a product with a different value proposition, it needs to create a Dedicated Team, at least for the affected portions of the design effort. For example, if Deere wanted to serve a new segment of customers, one that cared more about engine power than reliability, it would need to build a Dedicated Team with more numerous and more influential engine and drivetrain experts and fewer and less influential reliability experts.

OPERATING RHYTHM. What if Deere wanted to pursue a design effort of a different scale or duration? A product development team that is accustomed to five-year projects costing hundreds of millions will have a hard time simultaneously managing a five-month project costing tens of millions. To make such a shift, a company needs to build a Dedicated Team within which there are fewer engineers in each specialty and more frequent interactions across specialties. In fact, Deere has different product development teams that tackle much shorter and simpler tractor-like products, such as consumer lawn tractors.

By calling attention to these limits, we are not taking anything away from the individuals on Deere's product development team. They are all skilled and capable engineers. It is not at all hard to imagine them coming together to design a much wider range of products, from lawn mowers to locomotives. However, they are organized for one task and one task only—designing reliable, high-tech tractors for large-scale agriculture that have a system-level design like the 8030. To do anything else, they would have to reorganize. They would have to somehow dissolve existing work relationships and rebuild new ones from scratch.

Limitations Revisited

Again, the limitations imposed by work relationships are much more constraining than the limitations imposed by individual skill sets. You cannot ask person A and person B to change their work relationship to support the innovation initiative and to simultaneously sustain excellence in ongoing operations. A and B cannot have two work relationships at the same time.

Even if A and B do not have a Performance Engine work relationship, they will usually find it difficult to create one from scratch for the innovation initiative. This is primarily a matter of scheduling. To support the innovation initiative, A and B need slack time. And, if A and B are to work closely together, they need the slack time simultaneously. But if A and B do not routinely work together, their schedules are unlikely to be in sync. When A is free, B is busy.

Think of an initiative in your company that required collaboration between two or more people or groups that did not normally work together. What happened when ongoing operations became particularly demanding for one of the groups? Chances are that group dropped everything extra. Chances are the initiative lost momentum as a result.

This implies that the work taken on by the Performance Engine in support of the innovation initiative should *flow in parallel* to ongoing operations. That way, the addition of the innovation initiative only changes the volume of work flowing through the Performance Engine. It does not add new work flows or new work relationships, and it does not alter the work relationships that are already in place. Figure 1-1 shows one possible division of labor that meets these criteria.

We now look at three additional examples that show why three companies created Dedicated Teams to overcome the limitations imposed by the three critical dimensions of work relationships.

Depth: BMW Develops Brakes for Hybrid Vehicles

Chris Bangle, head of design at BMW, confronted the necessity to build a Dedicated Team when he faced an engineering challenge requiring a system-level design change. The challenge required deep work relationships in the Performance Engine where there were none.

Bangle was working to advance a technology known as regenerative braking. The notion is simple in concept and especially interesting for hybrid vehicles. Traditional brakes dissipate a vehicle's energy of motion

FIGURE 1-1

The work of the innovation initiative should flow *in parallel* with ongoing operations

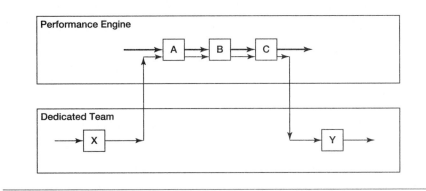

through friction, generating useless heat. Regenerative brakes, by contrast, capture the wasted energy and put it back to work. An electrical generator built into the brake recharges the batteries as the car slows.

The challenge of designing such a system was, of course, well within the capabilities of the individual engineers at BMW. However, the company's design processes were well established. In formal structure and process, *there was no reason for battery specialists to speak with brake specialists.* The two components were not linked physically in the car, and therefore the specialists were not linked in the organization.

Had an inspired visionary within either the battery or brake group tried to initiate an organic effort to build a regenerative brake, there may have been some progress. But those involved would have had to maintain their full-time Performance Engine jobs. Just to keep up, they would have needed to spend almost all their available time collaborating with their routine partners within the organization.

Specialization by component makes product design more efficient but makes the product design team less able to tackle system-level design changes. Bangle overcame the challenge by creating a Dedicated Team. He called it an "energy chain" team. It brought together all the component experts needed to create a new hybrid brake design and a new hybrid design process.

Power Balance: Electrolux Attacks
High-End Markets

Electrolux faced the necessity of a major transformation in product development in 2002. The European manufacturer of household appliances had, for years, served midrange customers with strong-performing offerings, albeit plain ones, that the company could produce efficiently through scale. Customers, however, were changing their priorities. They were gravitating to either the low-cost end of the market or the premium end. The midmarket, Electrolux's bread and butter, was disappearing.

To remain strong, Electrolux needed to change its product development agenda. That agenda, however, had been stable for decades. As a result, the product development team was very efficient—quite the Performance Engine. The company's engineers sought improvements in durability, efficiency, and price through the latest advancements in technology.

CEO Hans Stråberg chose to build a new capability to develop premium products. That would prove a major undertaking. The Dedicated Team upended many past company norms. In particular, it shifted power *away* from the formerly dominant engineering specialists who focused on technology and performance. Instead, the company empowered new "customer insight teams" charged with setting broad goals for each new product design effort.

Through elaborate diagnoses of customer wants and needs, the customer insight teams, staffed predominantly by outside hires, discovered some twenty subsegments at the premium end of the market. There was one major theme across all twenty segments: customers were interested not just in how well the products worked, but in how they looked in the home. To deliver on this new need, Electrolux built a second major new competence for the Dedicated Team, this one in industrial design.

While the need to shift power to new skill sets in customer insight and industrial design was clear, the details were not. For example, how should the company define work relationships between the existing engineers and the new designers? When in the product development process was input from the new industrial designers most crucial? These were problems Electrolux's Dedicated Team solved with time and experience.

Broad shifts in power are traumatic for any organization. Effecting the change at Electrolux was a multiyear effort driven by the CEO. By 2007,

Electrolux had doubled its frequency of new product launches, restored double-digit growth rates, and, according to a study by McKinsey & Company, more than doubled its total return to shareholders.

Operating Rhythm: Timberland Develops a Breakthrough Shoe for Trail Runners

By 2002, the footwear industry had developed a regular habit of creating new subcategories, particularly in outdoor and fitness. There was a special shoe for almost every occasion, from running to hiking to rafting. Through its annual planning and market analysis, the Timberland Company recognized the importance of the trend toward specialty shoes.

However, any project to develop new shoes for new specialties seemed likely to disrupt Timberland's well-honed product development team, which routinely delivered improved designs of existing products. The team worked under intense time pressure so that Timberland could introduce new offerings like clockwork, twice per year, at industry trade shows.

Therefore, Timberland created a Dedicated Team that it called the Invention Factory. The company expected the Invention Factory to operate on an entirely different rhythm. Instead of facing month-to-month pressures, it tackled multiyear projects.

Among the Invention Factory's first endeavors was a project to create a shoe for trail runners, who have unusual needs. Road runners worry most about minimizing the shock and strain on joints. The stress of each foot-to-asphalt impact accumulates and eventually results in injury. Trail runners, on the other hand, have a shorter-term concern: falling. Rather than trying to keep their upper bodies as motionless as possible, the way road runners do, trail runners constantly are shifting their weight and moving their arms to maintain their balance as they step on and over rocks and roots.

So, the Invention Factory set its top priority: to create a more stable platform for trail runners so they did not have to work quite so hard to stay on their feet. It was clear from the beginning that making incremental modifications to either hiking boots or running shoes was not going to yield a solution.

The design needed to start from a blank page, and that would take time. In fact, Timberland's trail runner would not be available to consumers until 2007. Helen Kellogg, director of business planning for the Invention Factory, oversaw a design process that ultimately involved several lengthy steps that were not part of the existing product development team's routines:

- Brainstorming meetings that lasted several days. The team took the time to consider design analogies from other industries. One important insight came from studying off-road vehicles, which had suspensions that allowed a great deal of motion under the vehicle while keeping the body of the vehicle stable. Timberland wanted similar functionality in its trail runner. In traditional running shoes and hiking boots, however, the bottom layer is quite rigid, and flexibility is in the midsole. Ultimately, the team reversed the design, so that the bottom of the shoe moved and compressed, while the rest of the shoe remained stable.

- More extensive exploration of possible materials, which required hiring engineers with deeper expertise in materials science and collaborations with experts in other industries.

- More extensive prelaunch testing, both by actual runners and in a biomechanics lab, where the company used testing equipment that could expose a shoe to the equivalent of hundreds of miles of running in a short time period.

- Lengthier and more careful interpretation of market feedback after launch.

Had Timberland asked the existing product development team to tackle the trail running project, these longer rhythm steps would likely have been squeezed out by more urgent priorities. As one executive said to us, "You can't ask the group that is in charge of today to also be in charge of tomorrow, because the urgent always squeezes out the important."

Indeed, it is very difficult for any team to be effective while trying to operate simultaneously at two completely different rhythms. Kellogg admitted that the most difficult transition for Timberland product developers moving to the Invention Factory was adapting to and taking full advantage of the longer operating time frames.

The Consequences of Overestimating the Capabilities of the Performance Engine

The preceding examples show that Performance Engine product development groups may be capable of handling all, some, or none of the product development tasks associated with an innovation initiative. Deere's Performance Engine tackled *all* product development, BMW's Performance Engine handled *some,* and Electrolux's and Timberland's Performance Engines took on responsibility for *none.*

Of course, most innovation initiatives span multiple functions, not just product development. It is critical to make the right choice about the division of responsibilities between the Dedicated Team and the Shared Staff in each.

The rules are the same in every case. The Shared Staff can take on tasks that are aligned with the Performance Engine's skills and work relationships. The Dedicated Team must handle everything else.

We have devoted this entire chapter to a single decision—how to divide the labor between the Dedicated Team and the Shared Staff—because it is consequential. When companies stumble, the recovery is difficult.

One company we studied, Analog Devices, Inc. (ADI), a $2 billion Massachusetts semiconductor company, learned from experience that it is hard to work around an organizational design that is a poor fit for an innovation challenge. A bit of background is necessary to understand its story.

Today, electronic gadgets are everywhere, from computers to cameras to cars. The semiconductor industry produces the components that lie at their core. The industry's devices come in many flavors, and two distinctions are important here. The first is the difference between digital and analog chips. Digital chips, such as the microprocessors in your computer, are terrific for abstract mathematics. Inside digital chips, everything is binary, either one or a zero, on or off. The real world, however, is analog, that is, continuously varying. Therefore, an analog chip is indispensible wherever there is an interface between a digital device and the real world. Computer peripherals, stereo systems, digital cameras, and instruments that measure, say, temperature or pressure, are all examples.

The second difference is between sequential processing and signal or real-time processing. Computer microprocessors are sequential. They execute all instructions they receive in the order that they receive them, no matter how long it takes. Signal processors, by contrast, do not tolerate delays. They give the best output they can in real time.

Founded in the 1960s, ADI excelled through its first three decades in designing and developing analog signal processors. The business grew very rapidly in the 1990s, driven in particular by robust growth in personal computers and their peripherals.

Despite the healthy growth, the company became concerned in the 1990s by the advance of digital signal processors (DSPs), which threatened to encroach on ADI's terrain. It no longer appeared safe for the company to focus overwhelmingly on analog chips. To protect the company and position it for the future, ADI's top leaders, Ray Stata and Jerry Fishman, chose to make a major investment in the development of a new DSP.

At the time, ADI's product catalog listed thousands of analog chips designed for specific applications. The company produced numerous new designs each year. There would never be a need, however, for thousands of DSPs. Just one could be programmed for a wide range of applications. Designing that one DSP, however, was a much bigger, costlier, and riskier project than designing an analog chip.

Organizing the Development Effort

ADI recognized the need to build a Dedicated Team to design the DSP. The company saw that even though its engineers were top notch as individuals, they were staffed and organized to build analog chips. Furthermore, the company's leaders recognized that they did not know exactly how to organize a DSP design team. They had never done it before.

For this reason and to share the capital costs of developing the processor with another company, ADI entered into collaboration with Intel. The partnership made sense from both sides. ADI knew signal processing but had limited experience with digital designs. Intel knew digital but had limited experience with signal processing. Jointly, the companies built a Dedicated Team. Roughly two years later, the initial design was complete, and the company began the commercialization effort.

Organizing the Commercialization Effort

While ADI saw the need to create a Dedicated Team to design the new product, it relied too heavily on its Performance Engine to commercialize it. ADI's Performance Engine had evolved to serve its core customers, technically sophisticated buyers who demanded cutting-edge, high-quality chips. Typically, customers were design engineers who understood exactly what they were looking for—an analog signal processor with clearly defined specifications.

The company was organized by product line. Each of several leaders of product categories focused on developing and commercializing technically superior components—ADI's traditional strength in the marketplace. There were deep work relationships *within* categories but much shallower relationships *across* categories.

ADI had a single sales force that distributed all products. Salespeople had engineer-to-engineer conversations with customers. They helped customers make certain they were getting what they needed and negotiated terms. Sales cycles were short.

All these organizational choices had worked well for decades, but DSP customers had different needs and behaviors. For example, rather than just buying the chip on spec, they demanded peripherals, design tools, and software all in one package. Many even expected a great deal of help in designing their own products. Some wanted to go so far as to offload the entire electronics design process to a single supplier.

In short, they demanded not just components but complete solutions. Cellular handset manufacturers, for example, wanted ADI to provide an analog chip, a digital chip, a memory chip, a radio transmitter, and more, all predesigned to work as an integrated package.

Buyers of DSPs also made much riskier decisions. Their selection of a supplier often implied a long-term commitment to compatible components and software. The decision was often made not by a design engineer but by a senior executive or even a CEO who expected ADI to think not just in terms of delivering a part, but in terms of helping the customer win in its own business.

Thus, the sales process was more complex, took longer, and demanded salespeople with a broader skill set. They needed to be able to engage customers both on business issues and on engineering issues. Furthermore, the sales process involved much more engineering work—assembling and integrating the components for a system-level design.

The commercialization challenge was not a good fit for the ADI's Performance Engine. It was not a match on any of the three critical dimensions of work relationships.

- *Depth.* ADI's Performance Engine operated in product category silos. That was the most effective way to serve its traditional customers. But to complete the systems design work that DSP customers were demanding, deep collaborations were needed.

- *Power balance.* ADI's organization vested substantial power in component-level engineers, but serving DSP customers well required that systems engineers and businesspeople take the lead.

- *Operating rhythm.* The process of selling a DSP can take several quarters, and ADI's Performance Engine operated on a week-to-week rhythm. Immediate priorities in the established business naturally squeezed out the attention that the DSP commercialization process required.

ADI learned from experience that its organization was not quite right. When complex, systems-level opportunities arose, the company was not as effective as it needed to be in demonstrating its full capabilities to customers.

The company attempted a few work-around solutions that were less than fully satisfactory. For example, DSP product category leaders became de facto salespeople even though they already had demanding full-time jobs. And to try to create more capacity for working with customers on their systems design efforts, some wrote job descriptions for new positions that, in effect, were sales positions. But getting those new positions approved was difficult since sales at ADI had traditionally been centralized.

As we completed our research at ADI, the company was redesigning its DSP organization to shift more responsibility to dedicated resources. The language would, of course, be different and more specific to the company, but in general terms and at a high-level, we would prescribe a Dedicated Team with a charter for selling and delivering solutions, not components. The Dedicated Team would be organized for long-cycle sales and for systems design, and it would be the first point of contact for customers who sought fully designed solutions. The Dedicated Team would purchase (through internal accounting transfers) components from ADI's existing sales force. In this way, the Performance Engine would be left to focus on the tasks it was designed for and excels at. ADI's Performance Engine would be able to treat the Dedicated Team much like it treats all its other customers.

The Dedicated Team Is Not the Innovation Team

Chances are that once you have decided how to divide the labor, you will want to give a name to one or both teams. Chances are that you will not choose our bland and generic monikers, Dedicated Team and Shared Staff. We offer only one small but important piece of advice. Since the Dedicated Team is purpose-built for an innovation initiative, it is natural to think of it as the "innovation team." But doing so leads to several problems.

The first is that it is just inaccurate. After all, in some cases, the Shared Staff does almost all the work. At BMW, for example, the division of labor was roughly ten/ninety. The Dedicated Team tackled just the regenerative brake design, while the Performance Engine took on the remainder of the design effort plus commercialization. Regardless of the split, the scope of the Dedicated Team's responsibilities is always narrower than the scope of the innovation initiative. The *project* is always executed by the *partnership*.

Also, calling the Dedicated Team the "innovation team" undermines the partnership. A relationship of mutual respect is unlikely if there is a perception that the Dedicated Team is uniquely innovative. The implication that the Performance Engine is *not* innovative will be heard loud and clear, whether intended or not.

To help sustain a healthy partnership, you, as the innovation leader, must be careful how you shape your identity. You may quite naturally be inclined to more closely associate with the Dedicated Team. But since you are a leader of the *partnership*, it is best that you are viewed as the leader of the project as a whole and not too closely associated with either side.

Revisiting the Overall Prescription

Now that we have described the partnership between the Dedicated Team and the Shared Staff, we will revisit the book's overall prescription. *Each innovation initiative requires a team with a custom organizational model and a plan that is revised only through a rigorous learning process.* This solution overcomes the fundamental incompatibilities between ongoing operations and innovation:

- Because ongoing operations are *repeatable,* while innovation is *nonroutine,* innovation leaders must think very differently about *organizing.*

FIGURE 1-2

The *partnership,* not just the Dedicated Team, executes the initiative

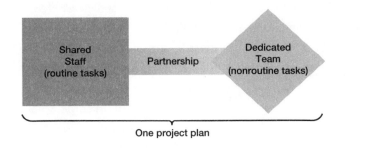

- Because ongoing operations are *predictable,* while innovation is *uncertain,* innovation leaders must think very differently about *planning.*

The custom organizational model is always a partnership between a Dedicated Team and the Shared Staff. The Dedicated Team addresses the first incompatibility by taking on the nonroutine portion of the effort. The Shared Staff takes on the repeatable portion, that is, those activities that are consistent with the Performance Engine's individual skills and work relationships. Depth, power balance, and operating rhythm are the three defining dimensions of work relationships.

The second incompatibility is addressed by the initiative's plan. Critically, the plan spans the entire initiative. It is the project team's plan, not the Dedicated Team's. (See figure 1-2.)

Note that while the Shared Staff cannot take on nonroutine tasks, it *can* take on tasks with uncertain outcomes. The appropriate division of labor between the Dedicated Team and the Shared Staff has nothing to do with uncertainty of outcomes. For example, consider BMW's hybrid car. The outcome of the entire new product launch was uncertain, not just the performance of the Dedicated Team's regenerative brakes.

Dividing the Labor: Observations and Recommendations

1. To execute an innovation initiative, build a partnership between a Dedicated Team that is custom-built for the initiative and a

Shared Staff that remains a part of the Performance Engine and maintains its existing Performance Engine responsibilities.

2. The Shared Staff should take on as much of an innovation initiative as it can. Be careful though. It is easy to overestimate the capabilities of the Performance Engine.

3. Performance Engines are designed for efficiency. However, the more efficient an organization becomes, the more specialized it becomes. The Performance Engine cannot simultaneously sustain excellence in ongoing operations *and* execute an innovation task that is outside the narrow confines of its specialization. If it tries, it will fail at one or both.

4. The limits of the Performance Engine's capabilities are defined both by the skills of its people as individuals *and* by the work relationships between them.

5. There are three critical dimensions of work relationships—depth, power balance, and operating rhythm. If an innovation task is inconsistent with the Performance Engine's work relationships on any of these three dimensions, it must be moved to the Dedicated Team.

6. The Dedicated Team is not the "innovation team" and should not be perceived as such. The innovation initiative is executed by a partnership between the Dedicated Team and the Performance Engine, and the entire project is managed through a single project plan.

CHAPTER TWO

Assemble the Dedicated Team

IN 1995, THE NEW YORK TIMES COMPANY launched its Internet business, New York Times Digital (NYTD). When it did so, it created a team with a custom organizational model. The Dedicated Team designed and built the Internet site, managed its daily operations, marketed the site, and sold ads. The Shared Staff enabled NYTD to leverage the *New York Times* brand and newspaper content.

By 1998, the team believed that it was performing quite well against its direct rivals, other newspapers. At the same time, the team was frustrated by the number of new-media opportunities that it was missing. For example, the entire industry responded slowly to the threat from Monster.com, the Internet alternative to recruiting through classified advertisements in newspapers.

The problem, in a nutshell, was that the Dedicated Team behaved like the Performance Engine. They even referred to their own operation as "newspaper.com." Only after a major organizational overhaul did the venture find its footing and put itself on a much more robust growth trajectory.

This common phenomenon can happen to you. Organizations are sticky. They struggle to escape the past. Even if you properly divide the labor, it is easy to build a Dedicated Team that acts like a Little Performance Engine.

A Dedicated Team will succeed only if it is able to overcome a phenomenon we call *organizational memory*. Of course, organizations do not have memory in the same sense that individuals have memory. What organizations *do* have is a tendency to create subgroups that mimic what already exists, even when the conscious intent is otherwise. This tendency is present in every company.

We'll start this chapter by offering a few simple principles for assembling the Dedicated Team—that is, picking the right people and organizing their efforts—in such a way that the team is able to overcome organizational memory. The principles we will offer are unlikely to surprise you.

What may surprise you is how frequently and how easily companies stumble. Though the principles are easy to describe, they are hard to follow. Thus, the bulk of this chapter will alert you to the pitfalls and explain how and why they have tripped up even the best companies.

We will conclude the chapter with three examples of companies that have built winning Dedicated Teams.

A Few Basic Principles

Here is how we advise you to assemble your Dedicated Team:

1. Identify the skills that you need.

2. Hire the best people you can find.

3. Match the organizational model to the Dedicated Team's job.

Let's go just one layer deeper into each of these recommendations. First, consider both specific skills and general skills that your Dedicated Team will need. By specific skills, we mean the individual know-how, capabilities, and experience that are *specific* to your innovation initiative. For example, Timberland recognized that expertise in advanced materials would be essential for its Invention Factory.

In addition, every Dedicated Team needs a more general set of innovation skills. A great deal has been written on the topic of how you identify innovators. Yes, they are creative, they question assumptions, and they come up with nontraditional solutions. Yes, they are able to draw on rich and diverse networks for ideas, they are tremendously ambitious, and they are comfortable when faced with uncertainty—both uncertainty in the outcome of the project and uncertainty in how their own roles and responsibilities will evolve.

These criteria are useful for *all* innovation endeavors, including start-up ventures. We add two additional considerations for innovation inside established organizations. First, having at least a few people on the Dedicated Team who have been through the process of building and shaping a new sub-unit within an established organization at least once before is helpful. Second, the most senior leaders of the Dedicated Team should be politically savvy and skilled at building partnerships. Managing the partnership between the Dedicated Team and the Shared Staff is tricky, as we will see in the next chapter.

Once you have identified the characteristics of the ideal candidates, hire the best you can possibly get. Consider all possible sources—internal transfers, external hires, even acquisitions of small companies.

Then, turn the individuals into a team, one that is *custom built* for the task at hand. Consider all aspects of organizational design, including reporting structure, decision rights, titles, job descriptions, work processes, performance measures, compensation plans, and culture. There are an infinite number of innovation projects and thus an infinite number of organizational models for Dedicated Teams. It is impossible to generalize, except to say that the Performance Engine's organizational model cannot be the default choice.

Innovation initiatives face a great deal of uncertainty. It may be difficult, at launch, to foresee the optimal way to organize the Dedicated Team. Therefore, you will want to be cautious about letting your organization set itself in stone too quickly. The instinct of the Performance Engine is to codify organizational structures and work processes as quickly as possible to maximize efficiency. That instinct can work against Dedicated Teams.

Overall, these principles are straightforward. Nonetheless, we have seen that companies frequently violate them. Indeed, if you are leading an innovation effort, you will face numerous pressures to do the wrong thing. If you bow to those pressures, you won't build a winning Dedicated Team; you'll build a Little Performance Engine. And your initiative will fail.

We now examine seven common mistakes.

Trap 1: Having a Bias for Insiders

By far, the most common pitfall is choosing too many internal transfers and too few outside hires. Because this trap is so prevalent, we will dedicate much more space to this first trap than to any of the remaining six. There are several reasons for the bias:

- *Pride.* Confident leaders in accomplished companies naturally believe that they can get the job done with the people they have.

They may even feel a sense of inadequacy in acknowledging that they need help from the outside.

- *Familiarity*. Most people making hiring decisions intuitively think about people they know before thinking about skills they need. If you have worked for the same large organization for many years, your network of professional contacts is dominated by insiders.

- *Comfort*. Hiring an outsider, especially for an influential position, portends change and feels threatening. Doing so promises to shake up the existing power structure.

- *Expedience*. Finding and transferring someone from the inside is usually faster. Most innovation leaders are eager to move quickly to be sure that they beat the competition to market. The last thing they want is to get bogged down in an exhaustive hiring process.

  Finding an outside hire for a Dedicated Team can be more taxing than routine hiring. Dedicated Teams often need skills that the company has never sought before. Therefore, the existing, well-honed recruiting pipelines may be of little help. Finding the best person for the job can demand a great deal of personal networking, or it may require building good relationships with new executive search firms.

- *Compensation norms*. Recruiting an outsider can be a particularly difficult challenge when the innovation effort takes a company into an arena in which its established and entrenched compensation policies no longer make sense. For example, during the dot-com boom, many large corporations that launched Internet ventures found their pay scales for IT professionals were inadequate.

- *A desire to give attractive opportunities to your own employees*. Employees are often attracted to opportunities to work on innovation initiatives. A success typically boosts a career. Hiring an outsider for a much-sought-after position can disappoint and demotivate existing employees.

These pressures to choose insiders can be difficult to resist. Too often, however, settling for insiders is settling for too little. It exposes the Dedicated Team to two risks—that it will be inadequately skilled and that it will fall prey to organizational memory.

The Risk of a Skills Deficit

Leaders of Dedicated Teams should always ask the question: if I were aiming to build the world's best team for the job at hand, would I hire *only* from my own company? The answer is usually no. For most Dedicated Teams, relying entirely on insiders leads to deficits in both specific and general innovation skills.

Many innovation initiatives, particularly growth initiatives, are intended to expand the boundaries of a business—to push it into new markets, to serve new customers, or to develop new technologies. To expand a business, you must expand your company's inventory of skills. You need Dedicated Teams with skills that you have never needed before.

Furthermore, large and established corporations are not typically awash with people who have general innovation skills or deep innovation experience. Many people are attracted to large companies precisely because they are not risk takers and they are not comfortable with ambiguity. Natural innovators, on the other hand, tend to seek start-up and small company environments.

We have seen several examples of innovation efforts in which the choice to hire outsiders was pivotal, including one at Harley-Davidson, the iconic American manufacturer of motorcycles. Most companies would be thrilled to have a brand as healthy as Harley's. Many of Harley's customers are loyal for a lifetime. But the brand was also a liability in the company's efforts to expand its customer base. Harley's community of motorcycle riders is so rabid and so tight-knit that it can intimidate newcomers.

The company sought innovative ways to create a more comfortable path into the Harley community for the interested but intimidated. Soon, the company was offering a range of new services for beginners, such as instructional courses, safety courses, travel and tour packages, rental programs, and consulting services to help new riders pick just the right model.

But how could a company that was historically focused on excellence in manufacturing develop and deliver high-quality motorcycle-related services? Some manufacturing-centric companies might have overestimated the importance of expertise in the motorcycles. Harley-Davidson, to its credit, recognized the even greater importance of experience in managing a services business.

Lara Lee, leader of the effort, went to great lengths to build a strong Dedicated Team that included many with deep services experience. She saw that Harley-Davidson's human resource team would have a hard time helping. It was already working overtime just to keep up with growth in the core business. Besides, it had little experience hiring the type of person that Lee was looking for. Therefore, Lee and her team directed the hiring process themselves. They worked outside the company's traditional recruiting pipelines, creatively finding new and previously unexplored avenues to identifying the right kinds of people.

If every company were equally aware of its strengths and weaknesses and equally committed to finding and hiring the best people available, its innovation initiatives would be much more likely to succeed. Harley's rapid growth in the current decade is evidence of the power of this approach.

When NBC and Fox joined forces to create Hulu.com, a rival to YouTube that offers branded and copyrighted content from the two networks, many critics snickered. They predicted that old media would never figure out the Internet, and that partnerships between competitors never worked anyway. The critics were wrong. By 2008, Hulu was earning more profit than YouTube.

The choice to hire outsiders proved crucial. Partners in joint ventures often jockey for power by seeking to place their own people in the most powerful positions. The founders of Hulu were smart enough to avoid this path. Instead, they sought outsiders with Internet technology expertise. The company chose an Amazon veteran, Jason Kilar, to be Hulu's CEO, and a Microsoft researcher, Eric Feng, to lead Web site development.

The Risk of Organizational Memory

A Dedicated Team composed entirely of insiders is likely to struggle with two particularly strong sources of organizational memory. The first of these sources is *instincts*.

Many businesspeople aspire to be as rational, data-driven, and deliberate as possible in every action. Nonetheless, everyone has habits, biases, behaviors, and thought patterns that have become second nature. These instincts are, of course, grounded in experience. If something has worked for you in the past, you are likely to keep doing it.

Experience is usually an asset for advancement within the Performance Engine, but it can be a liability for a Dedicated Team. Innovation initiatives are, by nature, deliberate departures from the past. The lessons of experience are therefore less relevant.

As such, leaders of Dedicated Teams are well advised to question their instincts. That's hard to do. People rely most heavily on instincts when they face uncertainty and pressure. Innovation involves large measures of both.

Instincts become stronger still when they are socially reinforced. If everyone on the Dedicated Team has been shaped by the same lessons learned from the same victories and defeats inside the Performance Engine, then the collective instinct will be even harder to escape.

The second strong source of organizational memory is *existing work relationships*. We saw in chapter 1 that work relationships define what the Performance Engine can and cannot do. So it should be no surprise that moving established work relationships to the Dedicated Team increases the likelihood of a Little Performance Engine problem.

Think about a colleague who you have worked with for a long while. Over time, you have no doubt developed any number of implicit understandings about how you work together. You naturally defer to your colleague on certain decisions. Your colleague defers to you on others. You routinely share certain information with your colleague and vice versa. You expect your colleague to take the lead in some meetings, while you take the lead in others. There is an established balance of power between you.

Now, imagine that you and your colleague are both transferred to a Dedicated Team. The business challenge changes, but, without any doubt, many of the implicit understandings about how you work together persist. Shifting the balance of power between two people who have a long-standing work relationship is particularly difficult.

Creating a strong Dedicated Team requires breaking down existing work relationships and building up new ones from scratch. Unfortunately, long-established work relationships are difficult to change. Dedicated Teams that are full of people who have worked closely together for years are almost guaranteed to become Little Performance Engines.

Outsiders and Organizational Memory

Most innovators whom we have interviewed over the years have experienced the problem of organizational memory. "We have got to stop behaving the old way" is a common refrain.

While many have observed the problem, actions to combat it are typically inadequate. Most try to attack the problem with encouragement and coaching—that is, by urging people on the Dedicated Team to think differently and behave differently every day. This effort is important, and it has some impact. But the problem demands a much more robust response.

There is no more powerful antidote to organizational memory than outside hires. Outsiders offer new perspectives. Their habits and thought patterns were shaped by other organizations. They are in a natural position to recognize and challenge long-standing, second-nature, instinctive assumptions. Furthermore, they have no past work relationships with anyone on the Dedicated Team. There are no existing work relationships to break down, just new relationships to form.

In multibusiness-unit companies such as Johnson & Johnson or Procter & Gamble, you could choose an "outsider" from a different business unit, someone who has no established work relationships with others on the Dedicated Team. However, even in multibusiness-unit companies, there are often certain conventions about work relationships that can be inadvertently imported to the Dedicated Team. At GE, for example, across all business units, finance has historically been a powerful function and marketing a relatively weak function. (Under Jeff Immelt's tenure, GE has strengthened marketing.) That is the type of legacy that could easily be transferred to a Dedicated Team composed of "outsiders" from multiple business units.

Rich Zannino, once the CEO of Dow Jones, said, "If you want to change the culture, change the people." That is right. He was talking about change in a broader sense, but the insight is on target for Dedicated Teams.

If you want to be 100 percent sure that you overcome organizational memory, the solution is the extreme approach. Include *only* outsiders on the Dedicated Team and then completely isolate it from the Performance Engine. A Dedicated Team's purpose, however, is not to overcome organizational memory. It is to execute part of the innovation initiative. To do so, the Dedicated Team needs both insiders and outsiders, and it needs a healthy partnership with the Performance Engine. The extreme solution is unwise.

We are concerned about Dedicated Teams that have fewer than one person in four coming from outside the company, as a rule of thumb. It is not generally necessary to recruit an outsider to lead the Dedicated Team, as Hulu did, but it *is* necessary to have some of the outsiders in influential positions. If the leader of the innovation initiative is an insider, then a healthy fraction of those reporting to the leader should come from the outside.

Hiring outsiders may be difficult. It may be time consuming, and you may be worried about getting to market first. Just keep in mind that your rivals, if they are to succeed, will likely face similar hiring challenges.

You may find that your company's HR team has no experience finding people with the required skills. You may need to rely on your own networking or find new executive search firms. Once you find an ideal candidate, you may have to work hard to persuade HR leaders to pay beyond normal compensation ranges.

You'll want to be ready to communicate forcefully about the need for outsiders. Some employees will be offended by the implicit belief that the company can't tackle the job on its own. Some will be nervous about the change that outsiders bring. Some will be envious of outsiders who took a position they wanted for themselves, or, worse, the employee base at large will get the misimpression that innovation is a job only for outsiders.

The message is straightforward: successful Dedicated Teams almost always include a combination of insiders plus outsiders with new skills and new perspectives. For all the difficulties and discomfort associated with hiring outsiders, the step is frequently pivotal.

From Individuals to Teams

You should be sure to avoid the first of the seven traps, defaulting to insiders, as you select individuals for the initiative. You want to escape the remaining traps as you turn your collection of individuals into a Dedicated Team. A healthy dose of outside hires counters some, but not all, sources of organizational memory.

As a result, Dedicated Teams must be assembled much like new companies being built from scratch. All need a zero-based organizational design. You may have heard of zero-based budgeting. It simply means that this year's budget cannot be justified based on last year's budget. Every dollar in the budget must have a clear business rationale.

Zero-based organizational design is similar. It simply means that no decision about how the Dedicated Team is organized—in particular, its definitions of roles and responsibilities, its reporting structures, and its work flows—may be justified with lazy rationales such as "that is how the Performance Engine operates" or "that is the way we have always done it."

Every organizational choice must be justified with a clear connection to the Dedicated Team's unique role.

To adopt a zero-based organizational design for the Dedicated Team is *not* to walk away from the benefits of being part of a large company. There is always a partnership between the Dedicated Team and the Performance Engine. It is the very ability to create such partnerships that gives established organizations such a powerful advantage over a start-up. It allows them to leverage powerful existing assets like brands, expertise, and customer relationships.

What the Dedicated Team should *never* try to leverage is the Performance Engine's way of organizing work. To ensure you avoid this problem, you must be aware of the six remaining traps.

Trap 2: Adopting Existing Formal Definitions of Roles and Responsibilities

A Dedicated Team can easily fall into working relationships that are similar to those in the Performance Engine, even if none of the people on the Dedicated Team have worked closely together before. That might happen, for example, if the Dedicated Team, as a matter of expedience, borrows existing titles and job descriptions from the Performance Engine.

We recommend that all Dedicated Teams take the following steps to help counter this problem:

Use new and unfamiliar titles. A title is much more than just a label. It is shorthand for a person's roles, responsibilities, and status. For example, the title of brand manager at a consumer products company like Procter & Gamble signifies broad general management responsibilities plus a great deal of authority. Using a long-established title invites people to assume that an individual has a similar role on the Dedicated Team as someone with the same title in the Performance Engine. But building a Dedicated Team is a process of breaking down and rebuilding work relationships. Using existing titles is a bad way to start. Instead, use new and unusual titles. Be creative. A new title encourages people to rethink their roles and responsibilities from scratch and to make an explicit effort to explain their roles to others. This is exceedingly healthy for a Dedicated Team.

Write new job descriptions. This may sound to some like a formality, but it can expedite the process of erasing the past. Dedicated Teams face a great deal of uncertainty, so new job descriptions are likely to be vague. The purpose of the exercise, however, is not to write accurate and detailed descriptions. It is to eliminate past knowledge about how work is divided between individuals. The exercise should not be delegated. Each member of the Dedicated Team should draft his or her own job description. The exercise is particularly important for pairs of people who worked closely together in the Performance Engine and are now both staffed to the Dedicated Team. Each pair must carefully examine the implicit assumptions regarding how they work together, eliminate those assumptions, and start a new work relationship from scratch.

Create a separate physical space for the Dedicated Team. Even in the age of instant Internet communications, regular face-to-face interaction between members of the Dedicated Team is invaluable. It expedites the process of breaking down and rebuilding work relationships. In the ideal situation, members of the Dedicated Team should all move from their existing desks into one shared space. Creating a new home for the team does not have to be expensive or complicated. One Dedicated Team we studied worked out of a rented trailer parked behind headquarters.

Trap 3: Reinforcing the Dominance of Performance Engine Power Centers

Most organizations have a function that is the power center. In consumer products companies, for example, the marketing function tends to be the most powerful.

When creating new subgroups such as Dedicated Teams, the natural tendency is that the power center remains the same, even if the need for a shift is obvious. In the late 1990s, for example, when established companies prepared to launch their first dot-com businesses, they needed to create Dedicated Teams with powerful IT functions. But how? If the company had been dominated, say, by salespeople for decades, then almost every sales-to-IT work relationship in the company was one in which the salesperson had more power. Augmenting their dominance, salespeople had more powerful personal connections within the Performance Engine.

You can achieve the needed power shift, at least in part, through formal and explicit means, such as through the hierarchy depicted on the Dedicated Team's organizational chart or through clearly delineated decision rights. Power shifts can also be effected through leadership choices. If the most powerful leaders on the Dedicated Team all have, say, an information technology background, then the IT function will naturally be powerful on the Dedicated Team even if it is weak in the Performance Engine.

Trap 4: Assessing Performance Based on Established Metrics

Evaluating a company's performance can be a complex and analytical process. Still, many companies want every employee to think about performance every day. Therefore, they simplify. They boil performance down to one or a few simple metrics. One services company we studied, for example, wanted every consultant to be aware of its business unit's revenues per employee.

Such an approach can bring focus, even more so if employee compensation is tied directly to these performance measures. However, the metric that is most meaningful for the Performance Engine is rarely equally meaningful for the Dedicated Team. Nonetheless, routine conversations about performance can easily carry over. The members of the Dedicated Team will talk frequently about how things are going—not just with each other but also with members of the Performance Engine—and the conversations will naturally gravitate to the company's most dominant performance metrics.

Even if the conversations are casual, they can have a dramatic impact on how the Dedicated Team behaves. Therefore, you must be sure that you identify the performance metrics that matter most for your specific innovation initiative. If you pay for performance, then you must ensure that incentives are in line with the Dedicated Team's objectives, not the Performance Engine's.

Trap 5: Failing to Create a Distinct Culture

By culture, we mean the commonly held assumptions a company holds about what it needs to do to succeed, such as "be frugal" or "put your client first" or "never sacrifice quality." One of the clearest windows into a company's culture is its collection of frequently told stories about what makes the company great. Often these tales are about the founder and a particularly bold or tense decision that shaped the company in an important way. In management consulting firms, these stories often remind young consultants to put their clients first. In news organizations, these stories often celebrate occasions in which the company was the first to break a big story.

These stories are powerful for the Performance Engine. But they can also shape behaviors within the Dedicated Team, even when the Dedicated Team has objectives that are inconsistent with the implied lessons of the company folklore.

Therefore, you should always take the explicit step of examining the company's culture and making conscious choices about what elements of the culture the Dedicated Team should and should not adopt. For example, consider a company that has always sold branded, premium products. If the company launched a Dedicated Team with a charter to formulate and commercialize a value-priced product for the developing world, it would need to work hard to eliminate the guideline, "always seek the highest possible level of performance," from the Dedicated Team's culture and replace it with, "watch every penny." The innovation leader would do well to look for opportunities to create and perpetuate new stories to reflect this new value.

One major caution: the Dedicated Team should *not* claim that it has a uniquely innovative culture. One Dedicated Team we studied decided that it should be fast-moving, creative, and anti-bureaucratic. Naturally, the Performance Engine did not appreciate the implication that it was slow, unoriginal, and rigid.

Trap 6: Using Existing Processes

Performance Engines are skilled at codifying each step in business processes and managing them for maximum efficiency. Formally established processes are perhaps the most obvious source of organizational memory.

Dedicated Teams, by nature, are faced with the difficult task of inventing new processes. When the processes look similar, it is tempting to simply copy the Performance Engine. However, if the identical process would truly work, then that portion of the initiative should have been assigned to the Performance Engine. There is never a situation in which the Dedicated Team should duplicate a Performance Engine process.

Trap 7: Succumbing to the Tyranny of Conformance

As a cost-saving measure, support functions are often under tremendous pressure to standardize everything. In human resources, finance, and information technology in particular, rigidly enforced standardization can be dangerous to Dedicated Teams.

Call these support functions if you will, but they are the holders of an organization's DNA, and they are extremely powerful in shaping the behavior of Dedicated Teams. Human resources controls titles, job descriptions, compensation policies, and recruiting policies. Finance shapes how performance is reported and evaluated. Information technology groups standardize and automate business processes.

Support function leaders who are intent on maximizing efficiency at all costs will make it nearly impossible for a Dedicated Team to overcome organizational memory. You must insist on being treated as an exception in these areas.

Building a Dedicated Team *Should* Be Uncomfortable

Again, the basic principles for assembling the Dedicated Team are straightforward: (1) define the skills you need, (2) hire the best people you can get, and (3) create a zero-based organizational model that is aligned with the Dedicated Team's responsibilities.

Nonetheless, companies constantly violate these principles when forming Dedicated Teams. They fall prey to organizational memory, and they create Little Performance Engines instead of Dedicated Teams.

We do not mean to trivialize the pressures that innovation leaders experience when forming Dedicated Teams. It is, without any doubt, easier and more comfortable to do the wrong thing and then try to coax the Dedicated Team to be different. But no matter how talented and persuasive the leader, no amount of coaxing will do the trick. Organizational memory is too powerful a force.

We have seen that while executives usually respond well to the recommendations in this chapter at an intellectual level, they are often uncomfortable at an emotional level, making such comments as: "That sounds expensive." "We have no history of taking steps like these." "A lot of people will resist."

Well, we never promised comfort. You can choose comfort, or you can choose to win.

———————

Let's now turn to three examples of companies that have assembled successful Dedicated Teams. These examples span a wide range—a new process innovation, a new product, and a new business. The same principles apply in each.

Process Innovation: Dow Jones Experiments with Circulation Marketing

In the late 1990s, the newspaper industry was awash in fear. Many in the industry anticipated that the rise of the Internet could only lead to the downfall of printed news. It still might, though as of 2010, printed newspapers were still ubiquitous. Regardless of the industry's fate, the Internet spurred a lot of experiments—some that failed, some that succeeded. There is a great deal to be learned from it all.

In about 2005, many industry insiders were aware that most readers did not suddenly make a complete switch to online news. Instead, most readers adopted hybrid reading habits. They preferred print for some content, particularly in-depth features and analysis, and the Internet for other content, especially breaking news. Some industry leaders thought it sensible to try to create an integrated news package in which the print and online products were distinct but complementary.

Dow Jones, now News Corporation, publisher of the *Wall Street Journal*, was one of the first to recognize the opportunity. CEO Rich Zannino saw that in addition to integrating its product, the company needed to integrate its organization, reinventing almost every business process.

The company suspected that integrating the processes for circulation marketing (selling subscriptions) was one area where major leaps in performance were possible. Unlike its industry peers, the *Journal* had always charged a subscription fee for access to online content. Both the print and online business units had their own distinct processes for selling subscriptions. No surprise, the print business sold subscriptions primarily through traditional channels (printed advertisements, call centers, and so forth), while the online team relied primarily on online marketing.

In 2006, as an experiment, the circulation marketing team at Dow Jones made an unprecedented subscription offer—one that the company would never have considered before. For a substantially discounted price, $99, anyone could purchase a one-year subscription to the *Wall Street Journal* that included both a printed copy of the newspaper each day plus full access to the Web site.

The results of the experiment were quick and unambiguous. The pilot was a success. Therefore, the company moved forward with a full-scale project to reinvent the process of selling subscriptions.

Based on the criteria described in chapter 1, the initiative clearly required a Dedicated Team. The existing work relationships in the Performance Engine were a mismatch on all three dimensions—depth, power balance, and operating rhythm.

- *Depth.* The Performance Engine was organized for specialization in either print or online products. But the innovation initiative needed close relationships between print and online specialists.

- *Power balance.* Print products were bigger and had a longer legacy in the company. As a result, the print groups were powerful. The innovation initiative, however, needed a roughly equal balance of power.

- *Operating rhythm.* The world of online marketing allows for very rapid feedback cycle. Try an online subscription offer today, and you can start evaluating its performance starting the very next day. Thus, the initiative called for a much faster operating rhythm than Performance Engine was accustomed to.

Building a Dedicated Team involves sharp change, and change is never easy. The leaders of the effort at Dow Jones were ultimately successful because they were willing to create and endure a great deal of discomfort and disruption as they brought print and online specialists together. Many described the year as the most tumultuous in the group's history. The tension was particularly tense because the company was so confident of success that it scaled down the old circulation marketing processes at the same time it scaled up its new one.

The company avoided the traps described earlier by taking the following specific steps as it shaped its Dedicated Team:

- *Hired outsiders.* To deepen its expertise in online marketing and online analytics, the company brought in experts from competing Internet publications. Insiders who struggled to adapt to the new mandates resigned or were let go. Several had been with the company for well over a decade.

- *Wrote new job descriptions.* Every job was redefined to span both print and online.

- *Shifted the power balance.* To effect the change, the company chose an expert in online marketing, Liberta Abbandante, to lead the team. The organizational chart of the Dedicated Team looked little like that of the Performance Engine. Most roles spanned both print and online. People who focused only on print had narrow, low-level responsibilities.

- *Identified new metrics and incentives.* Every employee had personal accountabilities that included both print and online goals.

- *Created a new culture.* The central value—"To succeed, we have to be platform agnostic."

- *Formalized new processes.* The team redesigned the process for designing, executing, and evaluating subscription offers. All offers were coordinated across all marketing channels. New steps were added for predicting and measuring the impact of each offer on all kinds of subscriptions.

Abbandante and her colleagues pushed these changes thoroughly and vigorously. One colleague commented, "The biggest lesson learned is just how hard it is to make a change like this. You really have to shake things up and challenge everything about how the organization works."

By early 2007, every offer, through every channel, emphasized the joint subscription offer (while still giving the option to choose print only or online only). All communications to readers conveyed the central idea that the *Journal* was a combined print and online package, and as a reader, you needed both. By the end of the year, individually paid subscriptions to the *Journal* were up by more than 9 percent, the biggest one-year jump in a quarter-century. This rise came without any drop in online-only subscriptions. Furthermore, by integrating print and online marketing processes, the company became much more efficient. The average cost of generating a new subscription dropped by 30 percent.

Product Innovation: Thomson Expands Its Information Services for Law Firms

You may have noticed that movies and television shows about the legal profession seem to be infinitely more popular than those about investment banking or management consulting. Apparently, issues of right and wrong with freedom or incarceration at stake are more dramatic than conflicts over profit and loss. But we digress.

Because of the ubiquity of the legal drama, you no doubt have a mental picture of a typical law firm office or judge's office. In all likelihood, that image includes stately bookshelves with rows upon rows of weighty volumes.

What you may not be aware of is why lawyers are so dependent on such extensive libraries. Only a fraction of laws in the United States are encoded in statutes passed by legislative bodies or regulations passed by appointed agencies. Wide swaths of law are rooted only in case law—the precedents of past legal decisions. In many states, for example, property laws and contract laws exist *only* in case law. Every legal decision becomes part of the accumulating body of past precedent. During the appeals process, in fact, almost all argumentation focuses on which precedents are most relevant to the judgment at hand.

Legal research would be both tedious and inefficient if not for the efforts of the publishing firms that serve the profession. They provide tremendous value by collecting, organizing, and publishing millions of legal documents from every jurisdiction around the country.

During the late 1990s, the legal profession made the shift from books to online research. For Thomson Corporation (now Thomson Reuters), the shift propelled rapid growth in its extensive online case law database, Westlaw. By 2000, however, almost all Thomson's customers had made the conversion to online databases. Growth suffered as a result, and the company began seeking new ways to expand. Several initiatives followed.

Historically, the company had focused on the needs of attorneys as they argued cases. In 2004, however, Thomson began exploring the possibility of offering new business information services that would help managing partners run their law firms more effectively, such as market intelligence or competitive benchmarking. Based on feedback from customers, the company zeroed in on a product that would be called Peer Monitor. The Internet-based product would collect data from law-firm accounting systems (with strict confidentiality understandings), aggregate the data, and create benchmarking reports that would enable a managing partner to compare his firm's profit margins to those of similar law firms.

Thomson already had strong relationships with law firms. Further, the Thomson brands, particularly the West imprint, were well respected, thanks to legacies in law firms that extended back to the nineteenth century. Thomson anticipated that it would have a much easier time selling Peer Monitor to law firms than a new venture would.

Still, Thomson saw that it needed a Dedicated Team to tackle almost the entire initiative, for several reasons. For starters, Thomson's Performance Engine lacked two critical skills at the individual level. The first was selling to high-level executives. Thomson sold to law firm librarians or law firm IT leaders, not to managing partners. The second was developing new software applications. Thomson was skilled at enhancing and maintaining its massive case law database, not developing unrelated applications from scratch.

Furthermore, the work relationships in the Performance Engine were a mismatch for most of the effort. For example, the power balance was not a good match. The most powerful individuals on the Performance Engine's product development team were experts in case law. For the new initiative, however, software development expertise and familiarity with the business of running law firms were much more important. In addition, the operating rhythm in the Performance Engine was quite different from that needed for the innovation initiative. The Performance Engine's IT team was attuned to ensuring that the case law databases, mission-critical for law firms, were operational twenty-four/seven. In that environment, it would be hard to give attention to a relatively small, longer-term, and less mission-critical project like Peer Monitor.

Thomson asked Allison Guidette, a marketing leader, to head the initiative full time and Alan Rich to be involved in its earliest stages, helping to shape the Dedicated Team. Rich was formerly the CEO of Elite, which offered accounting software to law firms. Thomson had acquired Elite in

2003. Guidette was able to leverage Rich's industry contacts to identify outside experienced software architects who had the skills and knowledge to lead the development of Peer Monitor. The company knew it would be extremely difficult to hire the level of talent needed into a publishing firm—and impossible without going well above Thomson's typical salary ranges. As a result, Thomson chose to hire a lead software architect on a temporary consulting contract and to outsource much of the work to outside software firms.

After a successful beta test, Guidette moved forward to build a sales team that was skilled in interacting with law firm leaders and knowledgeable of law, technology, and business. Guidette needed candidates with both JD and MBA degrees—expensive hires! Thomson chose to go beyond its standard salary ranges to make the hires.

The Dedicated Team showed no signs of struggling with organizational memory. This shows the power of outside hires in defeating the problem and the importance of hiring them into custom-defined roles. Only Rich and Guidette were previous Thomson employees, and Rich had come to the company via acquisition just one year earlier.

The company further minimized the risk of organizational memory in the way it evaluated the initiative. Rather than assessing progress on the basis of established metrics and standards used in the Performance Engine, the company evaluated Peer Monitor against its own separate and distinct business plan.

Although the Dedicated Team took on most of the task of building the new business, it did not work alone. It collaborated closely with the existing sales force to gain insight into the industry and into specific law firms. To facilitate introductions to senior law firm leaders, the Dedicated Team collaborated with Hildebrandt, a consulting firm owned by Thomson that served law firms and other professional services organizations.

Sales ramped up slowly in the first few months, but Peer Monitor had over fifty customers in its first year, and the company was soon able to raise its prices. The benefits of the success went beyond revenue and profit growth. Thomson was pleased to have a product that increased the strength of its brand with the most-senior law firm leaders. In fact, the company soon launched a series of additional new products for law firm leaders.

New Business Launch:
Lucent Starts a Services Group

In late 2006, Lucent signed the biggest network transformation services deal in its four-year history. A major telecommunications company in Europe had committed to a complex overhaul, one that would fully implement an Internet protocol for voice, video, and data. Lucent (now Alcatel-Lucent) would lead the effort, helping its client integrate equipment and technologies from Lucent plus several other providers.

It would have been hard to imagine such a deal when the company launched the services business four years earlier, in 2002. The dot-com bust had hit no industry as hard as it had hit telecom equipment providers like Lucent. A world of seemingly unlimited potential had become a battle for survival overnight. During the boom, Lucent had plans forecasting it would generate revenues as high as $40 billion within just a few years. The reality was a fraction of that, a shade under $10 billion.

Technological innovation had always been at the foundation of the company's success. The bust, however, forced Lucent to consider new models for growth. The services market appeared quite attractive. Telecommunications networks were being rebuilt for a new age. Each year, to get the job done, the industry spent more than $50 billion on consulting services and another $100 billion on internal projects.

Lucent already had a services group, but one with a narrow charter. Its mission was to support Lucent's core business, the network equipment business, by servicing its own products. Just by servicing its own equipment, however, the service team learned a great deal about equipment from *all* vendors. Telecommunications equipment was all interconnected.

In 2002, to get a sense of its readiness to enter the market for more complex services (not just servicing a Lucent switch, but transforming an entire telecom network), Lucent assessed the depth of its technical skills. It concluded its technical knowledge was deep enough to succeed.

Still, launching a network transformation services business was no fit for Lucent's Performance Engine. For one thing, the power balance was wrong for services. In the equipment business, technologists and product developers held a great deal of power. In a services business, the client relationship managers needed to have the most power. And, the rhythm of operations was much different. The telecom equipment business is a long-cycle, capital-intensive industry. Product development cycles and sales cycles span multiple years. The services business, by sharp contrast, has a week-to-week and month-to-month rhythm. Because of these differences, nearly the entire project needed to be executed by a Dedicated Team, one that partnered with the Performance Engine only to leverage the Lucent's brand and its relationships with existing customers.

An early leader of the initiative, Stef van Aarle, began assembling the team. Because Lucent was in the process of making deep cuts in its core business, there were plenty of talented people available and interested.

Van Aarle quickly discovered, however, just how difficult it is to retrain a product salesperson to sell services. Conversations with clients are much different. The challenge for product salespeople is to find customers who need the product and help them figure out how to deploy the product to get the greatest value from it. The challenge for a services salesperson is to broadly diagnose a client's problem and develop the best possible solution, one that might include both Lucent's equipment and a rival's.

The company's best salespeople were able to make the transition, but many struggled. As a result, Lucent began hiring salespeople from outside services companies. That proved a crucial catalyst in growing the business.

Van Aarle also tried to internally transfer some of Lucent's technology experts who were accustomed to long-term product development efforts. While some thrived under the intensity of client demands and the short-term pressures of the services environment, several left the company.

Finding the right people on both the sales and delivery sides was critical, but not quite enough to ensure that the Dedicated Team was effective. Lucent took several additional steps to shape the team in a way that ensured that it would defeat organizational memory:

- *Hired an outside leader.* Lucent made a critical hire, bringing John Meyer, a services veteran from EDS, in to lead the new business unit in mid-2003. Meyer subsequently hired more senior executives from services companies.

- *Built a separate human resource group.* The Dedicated Team's human resource group created customized titles, job descriptions, and compensation plans, using services units in other companies as models.

- *Elevated new performance measures.* In Lucent's products business, there was always the possibility of breathtaking profits from a runaway product. The company closely monitored return on investment by product. In contrast, services were by nature low risk and low return. Workforce utilization was a much more useful managerial measure.

  Lucent's leadership team also had to interpret head count differently. In the products business, managers constantly looked for ways to minimize head count. In services, revenues could only grow in rough proportion to the number of people employed.

- *Established new compensation and incentives.* Each employee who delivered services received a weekly report that indicated utilization rates and any bids from service managers for his or her time. Compensation was tied directly to performance.

- *Set up new processes.* In the core business, Lucent's employees were encouraged to share information frequently and freely. The Dedicated Team, by contrast, had to erect barriers to such information transfers, to protect client confidentiality.

By 2006, the services group was generating more than $2 billion in revenues. The benefits, however, were not just financial. The company discovered that the services business was a window that enabled better understanding of customers' needs. In time, Lucent's product developers adopted a broader perspective. They were able to consider the operation of entire networks and the complexity of integrating new products into them.

Lucent was also pleased by what it had accomplished organizationally. Competitors could usually duplicate a new Lucent product in less than a year. But to compete with Lucent in services, a rival would first have to succeed with a multiyear organization-building effort.

Assembling the Team: Observations and Recommendations

1. To build an effective Dedicated Team, define the skills you need, hire the best people you can get from either inside or outside the company, and create a custom, zero-based organizational model.

2. All companies, when building new subunits, are affected by organizational memory. Avoid building a Dedicated Team that acts like a Little Performance Engine.

3. Outside hires play a critical role on the Dedicated Team. They bring in needed new skills, and they help defeat organizational memory by challenging the instincts of insiders and by catalyzing the process of breaking down and rebuilding work relationships.

4. Create new and unfamiliar titles and write new job descriptions for everyone on the Dedicated Team.

5. The dominant function in the Performance Engine tends also to dominate the Dedicated Team. This tendency can be countered by formal hierarchy and decision rights and by leadership choices.

6. The Dedicated Team should define its own metrics, processes, and culture.

7. Support functions, especially HR, IT, and finance, must be willing to make exceptions to standard policies for the Dedicated Team.

CHAPTER THREE

Manage the Partnership

AETNA, THE $30 BILLION health insurer, had for decades served employers, particularly large corporations, by providing health benefits to their employees. But in 2005, one Aetna leader, Laurie Brubaker, was convinced that Aetna could no longer afford to overlook the market for individual health insurance policies. Nearly 45 million individuals in the United States were uninsured, and as many as 20 million more had inadequate insurance. As part of the strategic planning cycle that year, CEO Ron Williams asked Brubaker to piece together a business plan. The numbers were compelling, and Williams asked Brubaker to make building the business her new full-time responsibility.

By 2007, Brubaker's business had expanded to thirty states, serving 250,000 members. It was the second-fastest-growing business within Aetna. Brubaker and her team took pride in the fact that her business had both business impact and social impact—35 percent of sales were to the uninsured.

Brubaker saw that her initiative was outside the limits of Aetna's Performance Engine. It required new skills. For example, insurers estimate future medical costs for their corporate customers based on statistical methods. For individual customers, however, they can only do so on the basis of a medical evaluation. This requires experts of a different stripe. Also, reaching individuals required new capabilities, including Internet marketing.

While recognizing the need to build new skills, Brubaker also wanted to leverage several of Aetna's powerful assets. The most critical was Aetna's network of relationships with health providers, a network that a start-up would have taken several years to match.

Thus, Brubaker found herself faced with a common dilemma. She had to break far enough away from the Performance Engine to build an effective Dedicated Team. At the same time, she needed to remain close enough to build on existing assets. This frequently required Brubaker to persuade her internal partners—the Shared Staff—to prioritize her needs over the more immediate needs of Aetna's existing business.

Brubaker ultimately took several steps to strike the right balance. But her most important move was to maintain a positive tone in her outreach to the Performance Engine. She drew on a seemingly infinite reserve of enthusiasm. She spoke of her most critical friends in the Performance Engine as her internal partners. She was diplomatic. She constantly gave public recognition to the Shared Staff for their efforts. She wanted the Shared Staff to feel as if they were part of something important and part of a big success.

Not every leader can duplicate Brubaker's energy, but the essence of the example that she sets is easy to understand. Simply put, she saw *building a partnership* with the Performance Engine, not winning battles with it, as a central challenge in her overall endeavor. We think that Brubaker modeled the single most critical trait of successful innovation leaders inside large companies.

Take a Positive Approach

As an innovation leader, you must find a way to walk a narrow and delicate path. You must create a Dedicated Team that is purposefully distinct from the Performance Engine. At the same time, you must always treat the Performance Engine like a critical strategic partner. You must never alienate it, rebel against it, let your interactions with it drift into rivalry or hostility, or succumb to the temptation to view it as your antagonist.

This is tough. There are real and substantive conflicts between innovation and ongoing operations. Innovation often requires short-term sacrifice in order to achieve long-term gain. As such, the Performance Engine usually has good reason to fight you. It must, if it is to maximize quarterly profits.

You may have imagined, on the day that the investment in the innovation initiative was approved, that the battle for resources was over. But this is not the case. The battle for resources continues every day. You are likely to find frequently that you need more support from the Shared Staff.

Unfortunately, the members of the Shared Staff are not under your direct control. They also answer to the Performance Engine. And the Performance Engine has more power than you do. It is larger. Not only that, it has the stronger case for spending resources. Its arguments are more quantifiable, with shorter-term and more predictable returns on investment. You, on the other hand, can do no better than promise the possibility of a big, long-term payoff.

The odds are stacked against you and stacked against innovation. That is why a positive, persuasive and collaborative leadership style like Brubaker's is so important.

Get Help

But frankly, such a leadership style is usually insufficient. Innovation leaders generally lack positional authority. Even the most skilled need help from more senior executives.

They do not always get it. Senior executives are typically involved intimately with an innovation initiative only in the early stages, for example, in vetting the business plan. At this moment, when the funding decision is made, the difficult trade-off between innovation and ongoing operations, between the present and the future, is most obvious. Senior executives want to make sure that they are comfortable that the bet they are making is a good one for shareholders.

After that, the innovation initiative usually looks tiny compared to the Performance Engine. Some senior executives naturally shift almost all their energies back to the core business, imagining that they can hand off all responsibility for the initiative to the innovation leader.

That is unfortunate. In most cases, only a senior executive in the Performance Engine can effectively mediate ongoing conflicts. The most critical day-to-day role for the supervising executive, your boss, is to support you in your effort to make the partnership work.

Anticipate Conflicts and Deal with Them Proactively

While the most indispensible elements of the solution to ensuring a productive partnership are (1) the force of your positive leadership, and

(2) day-to-day engagement by the supervising executive, there is more that can be done.

There are many forms of conflict between innovation and ongoing operations. In the most successful partnerships, conflicts are anticipated and then either mitigated or neutralized—before they become real problems.

The many possible conflicts aggregate to three general challenges (see figure 3-1):

1. You will be competing with leaders in the Performance Engine for formally allocated resources.

2. You will be competing with leaders in the Performance Engine for the time, energy, and attention of the Shared Staff.

3. The Dedicated Team and the Shared Staff usually will *not* naturally work well together.

We dedicate the remainder of this chapter to identifying specific conflicts and responses in each of these categories. We conclude with three examples of companies that have made their partnerships successful.

FIGURE 3-1

The challenges of the partnership

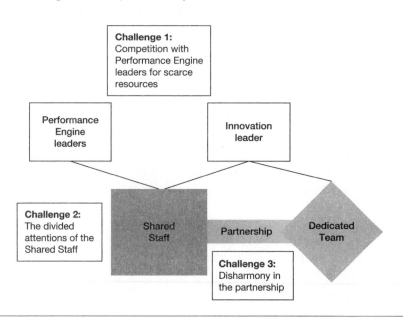

Challenge 1: Competition for Scarce Resources

In the early stages of your initiative, your requirements of the Shared Staff may consume only trivial resources by Performance Engine standards. But what if your initiative starts to succeed and your needs grow? You'll likely have to work harder to get the support you require. You may have to advocate for higher priority for your needs or even to push for a larger budget or a larger Shared Staff.

In this context, you are likely to find collaborating with Performance Engine leaders challenging. First, you will bring a much different perspective to the budgeting process. While you are comfortable with the uncertainty inherent in the innovation initiative, the Performance Engine is accustomed to relative certainty. Resources allocated to a given group or activity typically change by only a few percent each year. And, while Performance Engine planners will be under pressure to be as efficient as possible, you may be deliberately trying to increase capacity in anticipation of rapid growth.

Furthermore, there will be direct conflict. Performance Engine leaders will want their own projects prioritized. Or they may want to curtail total spending to maximize profits.

We studied a software company that illustrated the typical nature of this competition. The company created a Dedicated Team to develop a new product for a new market. The Dedicated Team took on nearly the entire initiative, but the innovation leader saw that he could utilize the Performance Engine's customer service group.

The head of customer service said to us, "I can handle their inbound customer service calls, no problem. I just need an accurate forecast of the volume of calls." When we probed, we discovered that by "accurate," he meant "within a few percent." But at that point, the initiative was in the early planning stages. All that could reasonably be expected was a guess within a factor of two in either direction.

Also, the leaders of the innovation initiative were eager to ensure that they had sufficient capacity to handle calls. They wanted the customer service group to make numerous hires and train them on the specific needs of the new market. Meanwhile, the head of customer service was under intense pressure to keep his costs as low as possible and the utilization rate of his customer service staff high. He did not see it in his interest to maintain spare capacity just in case the innovation effort rapidly took off.

We suggest the following principles for managing these conflicts.

- *Make* all *formal resource allocations to an innovation initiative through one plan and one process.* To see why this is important, imagine that you have already negotiated a total budget for your initiative with your CEO. As a result, spending within the Dedicated Team is uncomplicated. But for the Shared Staff, it is not so simple.

  Perhaps, for example, your initiative requires an IT systems development project and a modification in the manufacturing plant. Standard procedure within the Performance Engine is probably for such needs to be prioritized by functional leaders—the heads of IT and manufacturing in this case. They may, through reasonable and defensible logic, place higher priority on projects to support ongoing operations, or they may even refuse your request.

  Fragmenting resource-allocation decisions among multiple parties in this way can be a deadly mistake. It can result in a budget for an innovation initiative that is a disjointed mess.

  Although the CEO may have been thrilled to fund you, he may not be aware of these conflicts. They are often well below his radar screen. Resolving conflicts through a single document and a single process ensures that senior executives will remain involved.

  And they should *want* to be involved to ensure that short-term versus long-term trade-offs are aligned. It makes no sense to allocate capital to the long term from the top if the subsequent short-term trade-offs made elsewhere in the organization are overwhelmingly oriented to Performance Engine objectives.

- *The innovation initiative should pay fully for what the Shared Staff provides.* If you negotiate to expand the Shared Staff or to spend more in direct support of the initiative, then you should pay the bill. If what the Shared Staff contributes to the innovation initiative can be assigned a fair market value, you should pay full price. There should be no explicit price break for the innovation initiative just because it is an internal customer. Giving such a break just makes it more likely that Performance Engine leaders will deprioritize your needs.

- *The innovation initiative should pay for resources committed, not resources actually used.* If you overestimate your needs, you pay anyway. That way, Performance Engine leaders have less incentive to fight you, and you have full incentive to carefully consider the total costs of your plans.

- *Performance scorecards in the Performance Engine should, to the extent possible, be isolated from the uncertainty of the innovation initiative.* For example, in the software example earlier, the utilization rate of the customer service group could easily be recalculated to correct for the impact of an overcommitment of resources to the newly launched product. Such adjustments reduce the anxiety that Performance Engine leaders experience when spending on activities with uncertain outcomes.

- *Discuss contingency plans in advance.* The difficulty of forecasting the needs of an innovation initiative can easily lead to an underutilized or overtaxed Shared Staff. If the innovation initiative unexpectedly achieves explosive growth, the Shared Staff may not be able to keep up. On the other hand, if capacity is added just in case the initiative suddenly takes off, that capacity may lay idle. These mismatches can be large and uncomfortable by Performance Engine standards. To sustain a healthy partnership, responses to these possibilities should be discussed in advance.

Challenge 2: The Divided Attentions of the Shared Staff

Even if you are successful in winning formally allocated resources, it may not be enough. The resources actually expended on the innovation initiative are subject to the daily choices of the individuals on the Shared Staff.

By necessity, the partnership is between a group working on the initiative full time (the Dedicated Team) and one that is working on it only part time (the Shared Staff). Thus, each member of the Shared Staff chooses the fraction of his or her time that he or she will dedicate to the initiative. More powerful members of the Shared Staff may also control the extent to which the innovation initiative is able to leverage valuable Performance Engine assets such as a brand or a customer relationship.

You have to win not just formal resource battles but the hearts and minds of the Shared Staff. You need their time, their energy, and their attention. Getting it can be hard. To the Dedicated Team, the innovation initiative is *everything*. To the Shared Staff, it is only *one* thing. They might even view it as a distraction.

Motivating the Shared Staff is not always hard. In some cases, the Performance Engine is struggling to sustain high performance and sees the innovation initiative as the best chance to get back on top of its game. In such cases, your job is much easier.

But in other cases, you'll find yourself fighting the intense short-term pressures within the Performance Engine. Making matters more difficult, the individuals on the Shared Staff typically have stronger loyalties and stronger formal ties to leaders in the Performance Engine, especially if they are supporting the innovation initiative with only a small fraction of their time.

Consider a typical scenario in which a company charters a Dedicated Team to develop a new product. Because the product is designed for existing customers, the company plans to sell it through the Performance Engine's sales force. In such a scenario, the entire initiative is at the mercy of decisions made on the front lines, by individual salespeople.

If the innovation leader is lucky, the salespeople will give plentiful attention to the new product because they are delighted to have something new to talk about with their customers. This situation is hardly guaranteed however. Alternatively, the salespeople may find that it takes much longer to explain the new product compared to existing products. They only have limited time with each customer, they have a sales target they have to hit, and they want to maximize their income from commissions. Naturally, they will emphasize the products that they can sell quickly. Another possibility is that the salespeople will worry that selling the new product will endanger their reputations with customers. If the new product fails, it might put future sales of existing products at risk.

Such situations are not limited to sales. They can appear in most any function. When you use a Performance Engine manufacturing facility, for example, you may rely on a day-to-day scheduler to work in production runs for your new product. And when you need input from a group of technical experts in the Performance Engine, they must choose to make time for you.

Get Assistance from Above

Your task is much easier if the supervising executive is fully behind you. You should be sure the supervising executive understands that for an innovation initiative to succeed, the decision to prioritize the long term over the short term needs to be made not just once but repeatedly—and not just at the strategic planning level, but at operating levels and even at the individual level. You need the supervising executive to become a constant advocate for the long-term view.

Senior executives are most effective in their advocacy when they anticipate the intensity of the competition for the time and attention of the Shared Staff. The fight will be heightened, for example, in the Performance Engine's busy seasons. Conflicts are also acute when capacity is fixed, as it is when an innovation initiative is utilizing a Performance Engine manufacturing facility that is operating at full load. In such situations, there is a clear one-for-one trade-off between innovation and ongoing operations.

The challenge of attracting the energies of the Shared Staff is most difficult when there are substantive reasons to believe that the innovation initiative poses a direct threat to the Performance Engine's ongoing health or survival. Specifically, the Performance Engine may worry that the innovation initiative will either weaken existing assets or cannibalize ongoing operations:

- *Weaken assets.* The Performance Engine is protective of its assets, as it should be. One particularly vulnerable asset is an established and powerful brand. As one executive said to us, a great brand takes years to create and seconds to destroy. Also vulnerable are relationships with customers, partners, or suppliers.

- *Cannibalize.* The Performance Engine is likely to resist any innovation initiative that threatens to replace an existing process, product, or service (as opposed to promising to expand a company's activities). In such cases, some in the Performance Engine may fear that their incentive compensation is at risk or, worse, that they will lose their jobs.

When threats like these exist, resistance is likely to be spirited and emotional—and often deadly for the innovation initiative. For you to have any chance at success, senior executives must stand behind their choice to prioritize the distant over the immediate every day. They must argue that while the threats to ongoing operations are real, moving forward with the innovation initiative is still the better long-run choice for the company as a whole. If there are risks of damaging a brand or customer relationships, then the company must minimize those risks while supporting the initiative. And if the success with the initiative does in fact make some aspects of ongoing operations obsolete, the argument must be that those operations were bound to become obsolete anyway. *Someone* is going to capture the innovation opportunity.

These arguments are obvious, but that does not mean they will be readily accepted, especially if employees fear for their jobs. When practical, it may be worth gathering data to actually measure the extent of the threat. Fear can easily outpace reality. In one company we studied, there was high anxiety that a new offering would cannibalize the company's core product. The new offering, however, was only an indirect substitute for the existing one. The data proved that far from cannibalizing, the new product was reaching new customers and expanding the market for *both* products.

Additional Tools for Shifting Attention to Innovation

Time is scarce for senior executives. They may find it desirable to multiply the power of their interpersonal influence by also using incentives to shape the behavior of the Shared Staff. The incentives can be created at either the P&L level or the individual level:

- *Internal transfer payments.* When your initiative pays for the help that it receives from the Shared Staff, you get higher priority. In fact, you may even be treated like a customer instead of like a distraction. In practice, this means estimating the total time that members of the Shared Staff spend supporting the innovation initiative. Precisely measuring their contribution is unnecessary. The symbolism is more important than amount of the charge.

- *Special targets or added bonuses.* Individuals will shift more attention to the innovation initiative if they have a specific innovation target to achieve or if they can earn a bonus. For sales forces, a higher commission rate might be paid for the new offering. Or, where a Dedicated Team sales force is relying on support from a Shared Staff sales force, say, to approach existing customers, some companies have paid a double commission, to both Dedicated Team and Shared Staff salespeople.

Challenge 3: Disharmony in the Partnership

Even if you are successful at winning the energies of the Shared Staff at first, there are inevitably forces that push the partnership toward an "us versus them" rivalry. Left unchecked, such a rivalry can sink an innovation initiative.

The rivalry is fueled by the necessity of creating a Dedicated Team that is organized and operates much differently from the Performance Engine. But the worst possible cure is to eliminate these differences. Doing so will only turn the Dedicated Team into a Little Performance Engine. The differences *must* be sustained.

The better response is to anticipate the specific resentments that are likely to arise, to be alert to their presence, and to go out of your way to defuse them in advance. The most common tensions center on specific differences, real or perceived, between the Dedicated Team and the Shared Staff:

- *Perceived skill.* Even if you do nothing to fuel the perception, the notion that the Dedicated Team is uniquely innovative or otherwise superior may start to circulate, or worse, a perception that "winners" are staffed to the Dedicated Team while "losers" remain in the Performance Engine.

- *Perceived importance to the company.* This resentment can work in either direction. We have seen cases in which the CEO talks so much about innovation that those running ongoing operations feel diminished. We have also seen cases in which a Dedicated Team is maligned as a quirky group running a useless experiment. Either way, the partnership is undermined.

- *Performance assessment.* Innovation initiatives are not properly evaluated by the same metrics, standards, or forms of accountability as ongoing operations. Most obviously, the Performance Engine is expected to earn a profit each quarter, while innovation initiatives typically lose money before making money.

- *Compensation.* To build a winning Dedicated Team, a company may need to recruit for skill sets it has never needed before. It may need to pay outside of company norms to get them.

- *Roles and responsibilities, structure, and culture.* The Dedicated Team is different by design. Though these differences are purposeful, they can contribute to a general lack of trust.

- *Who should have decision rights.* If the Performance Engine has exercised full control of a certain operation for years and suddenly the Dedicated Team demands shared control, the Shared Staff will feel threatened and will resist.

As you can see, there are many reasons that the Performance Engine and the Shared Staff in particular may resent the Dedicated Team. In a nutshell, "We don't like you because you are different, you seem to think you are superior, you have more fun, you get all of the glory, you get special treatment, and on top of all that, you are invading my turf."

In trying to defuse these tensions, you always want to make clear and positive arguments about why the differences are necessary—not because the Dedicated Team is superior or innovative and deserves special treatment, but because the Dedicated Team has a unusual job, one for which the Performance Engine was not built. At Aetna, Brubaker constantly reminded people of the deep differences between insuring individuals and insuring corporations.

We offer five additional principles that can help to ensure a vibrant partnership:

1. *Make the division of responsibilities as clear as possible.* Partnerships are more likely to thrive when both sides understand their roles. Misunderstandings are most likely when there is a complete handoff of responsibility from one partner to the other, as when the Dedicated Team develops a product and the Shared Staff commercializes it. To ensure a clean handoff, it is sensible, if possible, to overstaff during the transition period.

2. *Go out of your way to reinforce the common values that the Performance Engine and the Dedicated Team share.* Innovation leaders need to frequently reinforce how the Dedicated Team needs to be different. But it is a mistake to reinforce *only* the differences. There are always at least a few commonalities. For example, both sides have an interest in the long-term success of the company as a whole. And, both typically share commitments to such ideals as integrity and teamwork.

3. *Select* insiders *for Dedicated Team roles that demand heavy collaboration with the Shared Staff.* Until now, we have emphasized the value of outside hires. Outsiders help the Dedicated Team by bringing critical new skills and by catalyzing the process of breaking down existing work relationships and building new ones *within* the Dedicated Team. But work relationships *between* the Dedicated Team and the Shared Staff are also important. This is where insiders play a crucial role. Insiders who have established relationships and deep familiarity with the Performance Engine can build a successful collaboration more easily.

4. *Locate the Dedicated Team near critical members of the Shared Staff.* Collaboration is easiest with face-to-face interaction. Those members of the Dedicated Team who partner most frequently with the Shared Staff are best located nearby, say, in the same city. Face-to-face interaction *within* the Dedicated Team is also very important. So, the Dedicated Team needs its own separate space, but it does not have to be far away.

5. *Reinforce the importance of being able to collaborate across organizational boundaries.* A particularly strong reinforcement is a specific rating of this skill on individual performance reviews. If someone understands that her promotion depends on her ability to partner, then her behavior is likely to change.

In three of the companies we studied, a healthy partnership between a Dedicated Team and a Shared Staff was a critical success factor. One example is a process innovation, one a product innovation, and the third a new business. The same principles apply in each.

Process Innovation: A More Complex Sales Process at Dow Jones

Years ago, the formula for a winning advertising campaign was simple: shoot a creative and memorable thirty-second advertisement and then pay to run it during prime time on a major network. But by 2003, the formula had become more complex. Consumers had an overwhelming number of media choices. There were countless cable television channels and Web sites catering to ever-smaller subsegments of the population. As a result, many in the advertising industry believed that the most powerful advertising campaigns were not necessarily the most creative and memorable, but the ones that were best integrated across a wide variety of media. That way, consumers were exposed to a message repeatedly, no matter where they went.

The notion of an integrated campaign seemed powerful, but for established advertising agencies and media companies alike, designing and delivering an integrated campaign was a decidedly unnatural act. The difficulty was organizational. For decades, people in the advertising and media industries had specialized by medium. There were TV people, radio people, and print people. Even within companies that operated across multiple media, there was little history of collaboration.

In 2004, Rich Zannino, CEO of Dow Jones, funded an effort to build a new capability for integrated campaigns after a successful pilot that included Dow Jones's newspapers, magazines, and television stations. Matthew Goldberg, a recent hire with experience in integrated campaigns, led an effort to build a new offering that the company dubbed Dow Jones Integrated Solutions (DJIS).

The depth and operating rhythm of work relationships in Dow Jones's Performance Engine was no match for integrated sales. Salespeople interacted primarily with other salespeople in their media specialty, but DJIS needed heavy cross-media collaboration. Also, the Performance Engine sales force was accustomed to negotiating terms and closing deals day to day and week to week. DJIS's sales cycle would be much longer, because it was harder to sell an entire campaign than it was to sell advertising space. Conversations with clients were more collaborative and less transactional.

Recognizing these differences, Goldberg built a Dedicated Team. Rather than drawing on organizational conventions within Dow Jones, he drew on his experience managing integrated sales for a prior employer. He defined new roles and responsibilities, and then sought the best people for the job. Some came from inside Dow Jones, some from outside.

Goldberg built a strong Dedicated Team, but it could not succeed in isolation. Most critically, it needed a close partnership with the company's existing sales forces so that it could build on existing client relationships.

Goldberg felt, in fact, that there was no way that DJIS would succeed if the Dedicated Team alienated Dow Jones's largest sales force, that of the *Wall Street Journal.*

The relationship with the Shared Staff was delicate. Some of the *Journal's* salespeople viewed DJIS as competition for commissions. Others were concerned that a DJIS campaign that disappointed a client would damage a relationship that they had nurtured for years.

In addition to exerting the force of his own persuasive leadership style, Goldberg took the following steps to make it more likely that the *Journal* sales force would dedicate its scarce time and energy to DJIS:

1. *Located the Dedicated Team near the* Journal's *sales staff.* This ensured there would be frequent face-to-face interactions that would build trust.

2. *Respected the Shared Staff's limited free time.* Moving quickly was the only way for the *Journal's* salespeople to hit their targets. Once they made a sale, they moved on to the next client right away. Therefore, Goldberg kept the role of the Shared Staff clear and limited. He made every effort to avoid distracting them postsale.

3. *Anticipated and minimized fear.* To counter fears that DJIS might harm a valuable relationship with an important client, Goldberg instituted a policy that no DJIS salesperson would ever call on a client without working through existing client leads on the Shared Staff.

4. *Deployed insiders in key positions.* By attracting a former *Journal* sales manager to work on the Dedicated Team, Goldberg took advantage of existing work relationships to bolster the partnership. Because the individual already had credibility within the *Journal* sales team, he was able to help build and sustain trust and to prevent the onset of an us-versus-them mind-set.

Goldberg had help from Zannino and other senior executives, who frequently advocated for DJIS. For example, they:

- *Formed an oversight board.* To ensure that DJIS was able to identify and capitalize on all opportunities for integrated sales no matter where they arose, Zannino created an Integrated Solutions Council that included the heads of sales and marketing for every media property the company owned plus senior executives from head-quarters. This was both practical and symbolic. Everyone in sales and marketing understood that Zannino wanted DJIS to succeed.

- *Celebrated DJIS victories throughout the company.* To signal DJIS's importance to the company, Zannino highlighted its big wins in broad Dow Jones communications.

- *Used the power of bonus compensation.* Zannino approved a special bonus that was awarded whenever a member of the Shared Staff contributed to a DJIS sale.

DJIS had proved successful to everyone's satisfaction by 2006, earning roughly $25 million in incremental revenues. Goldberg was promoted to a new position in Dow Jones's new ventures group.

Product Innovation: WD-40 Seeks to Expand Its Product Line

In 1953, in a lab in San Diego, California, the tiny Rocket Chemical Company labored to develop an ideal rust-prevention solvent for the aerospace industry. A few employees snuck product samples out of the lab and experimented with them at home.

The illicit in-home testing became inspiration for business expansion. Soon the company relaunched its water-shedding concoction as a consumer product that it dubbed WD-40. (According to company lore, WD stands for water displacement, and it took forty attempts to get the formula just right.) Before long, the company had adopted the same name. Consumers constantly found new uses for the product, such as eliminating squeaks from door hinges. By 2009, the company's Web site listed over two thousand possible applications.

On the strength of just one product and its seemingly inexhaustible popularity, the WD-40 company grew to nearly $150 million in revenues by 1997. In that year, however, CEO Garry Ridge began seeking new sources of growth. After a string of acquisitions, Ridge turned his attention to generating organic growth through a broader product development agenda.

Until then, WD-40's marketing team had led all new product development efforts, usually short-term projects that sought to improve, renew, or repackage existing products. Now, Ridge wanted to invest in multiyear, more groundbreaking efforts. Ridge created a Dedicated Team that he called Team Tomorrow to design and develop the breakthrough new products. He left commercialization in the hands of the Performance Engine.

Team Tomorrow was distinct. Stephanie Barry, who led the team, hired research scientists from the outside and developed new collaborations with outside partners. One of the team's early successes was the WD-40 No-Mess Pen, a way to more easily dispense small quantities of WD-40 in tight spaces. The project confronted the team with unfamiliar technical challenges that required new expertise in pen technology and the chemical interactions between WD-40 and plastics.

The No-Mess Pen went on to be a major success and a major victory for Team Tomorrow. Customer feedback was exceptional. The product was particularly attractive to women, a segment the company had not previously targeted.

The company consolidated lessons learned from the positive experience and focused on repeating the success. There were several additional new products in Team Tomorrow's pipeline. Notable aspects of the company's approach included:

- *A leader focused on collaboration.* Despite the inevitable conflicts, Barry viewed the Performance Engine product development and marketing teams as critical partners.

- *Steady advocacy directly from the CEO.* Ridge constantly talked about the No-Mess Pen and even carried a prototype wherever he traveled. As a result, it was widely understood that Ridge wanted to prioritize the long term over the immediate.

- *A clear division of responsibilities between Team Tomorrow and the Shared Staff.* The company developed a seven-stage product development process. Team Tomorrow led the first four stages. The Shared Staff (the Performance Engine's marketing team) managed the last three.

- *Extra resources on the Shared Staff.* The company added new staff in marketing, including a new senior leader, to ensure that the team had sufficient bandwidth to commercialize the products coming from Team Tomorrow's pipeline while staying on schedule with the Performance Engine's original product development agenda.

- *An effort to gather data to assess the extent of cannibalization.* The company's analysis showed that the No-Mess Pen generated purely incremental sales, which diminished fears in the Performance Engine.

- *Emphasis on collaboration across organizational boundaries.* The relationship between Team Tomorrow and the marketing group was challenging at first, but the CEO's heavy emphasis on collaboration helped the two groups come together.

- *Close coordination in planning.* After experiencing bottlenecks in getting early products to market, Team Tomorrow developed a practice of going out of its way to collaborate with the Performance Engine during the planning process. And, it included marketing leaders in weekly project review meetings.

Adjacency Innovation: Business Model Expansion at Infosys

Since its founding in the early 1980s, Infosys's primary offering has been developing custom software for corporate clients. The company's founders had pioneered the concept of serving clients in the developed world from India, where talented software engineers earned substantially lower wages. The story of the company's meteoric rise was legendary in India.

But Infosys aspired to deliver a much broader range of services. As part of the expansion effort, Infosys launched a new unit, Infosys Consulting, in 2004. The new unit offered IT-related advice to business executives (as opposed to technical services for IT executives). Its offering included developing detailed specifications for major investments in new IT systems. This connected nicely with Infosys's core business. The existing service teams could follow by actually building the new systems for the client.

Because of the deep differences in skill sets and work relationships in consulting organizations versus software development organizations, Infosys built a Dedicated Team to execute most of the effort and built the team from the ground up. Infosys hired Steve Pratt, an industry veteran from Deloitte, to lead Infosys Consulting. Rather than looking to Infosys for an organizational model, Pratt drew on his experience in the consulting industry to define roles and responsibilities for the Dedicated Team. In addition, working with Infosys's senior team, he tailored a scorecard to his unique business, rather than relying on Infosys's established metrics and standards. For example, throughout its history, Infosys had closely monitored the fraction of its work that took place in India instead of at the client site. The target was at least 75 percent. But consulting teams needed more face-to-face interaction, so Infosys Consulting set a lower target.

While Pratt's Dedicated Team was much different from Infosys, he needed deep partnerships with it. He needed to sell to the same clients, and he needed to closely coordinate service delivery where Infosys and Infosys Consulting were executing related projects.

Infosys's client leads (the senior leaders responsible for all activities at a particular client) had plenty of reasons to resist the push to sell the new consulting services. Time was scarce, and selling a new service was harder than selling one that had a proven track record. Further, some client leads had nearly all of their professional reputation tied to success with a single client. Naturally they worried that Infosys Consulting might disappoint the client. Some also found Infosys Consulting's involvement threatening because the new unit needed to build relationships at higher levels in client organizations.

Pratt diminished tensions by spending as much time as necessary talking to Infosys client leads. The conversations focused on anticipating possible client scenarios and envisioning how to collaborate in each. Pratt was persuasive but also humble.

Because face-to-face meetings were hard to arrange in an organization spread across the globe, building trust was challenging. However, once Infosys Consulting delivered its first few successful client engagements, its credibility rose dramatically. Soon, it was flooded with new opportunities.

Pratt benefitted from the heavy support of the company's senior leaders, who recognized the danger of leaving Infosys Consulting to sink or swim entirely on its own. Chief executive Nandan Nilekani believed his explicit patronage was necessary to overcome natural skepticism of new services. All new business units at Infosys reported directly to the senior team, alongside established business units that were much larger. Infosys Consulting also had its own board of directors, a group that overlapped with Infosys's board.

Beyond direct advocacy, Infosys's senior management team altered incentives. For example, the company set specific revenue targets for both the core business and Infosys Consulting at every client. Further, when the partners collaborated on a sale, both sides were rewarded. Both units accrued revenues on internal scorecards and client leads in both units earned compensation.

In delivering services, Infosys Consulting tried to divide responsibilities between the Dedicated Team and the Performance Engine as clearly as possible, but it was not easy. A general guideline—that the consulting unit worked on business problems, while the established unit focused on technical problems—left plenty of room for interpretation. Therefore, the company deliberately overstaffed the handoffs to ensure that they were smooth. Also, the company's senior leaders practiced a philosophy of mutual accountability. If anything went wrong at the transition, both sides were held responsible.

Where conflicts arose between new and established units, Pratt always tried to ground resolutions in considerations that were aligned with the long-term interests of the client. Infosys's senior leaders were also involved, reinforcing the enduring values that the entire company shared, such as integrity, teamwork, and humility.

Infosys grew from $40 million to $400 million between 1996 and 2001 on the strength of its original business—software development. Thanks to the company's aggressive service expansion, including Infosys Consulting and several other units, the stunning growth rate continued. The company reached $4 billion in revenues in 2008.

Managing the Partnership:
Observations and Recommendations

1. The organizational model for an innovation initiative is always a partnership between a Dedicated Team and a Shared Staff.

2. The most critical characteristic of successful innovation leaders is that they take a positive, persuasive, and collaborative approach in their interactions with the Performance Engine.

3. To maintain a healthy partnership, even the best innovation leaders need help from above. Conflicts with the Performance Engine are frequent and can be intense. And, the innovation leader usually has little positional power compared with the Performance Engine leaders with whom there is conflict.

4. Both the innovation leader and supervising executive must attend to the health of the partnership at all times, anticipating, moderating, and mediating tensions and conflicts.

5. Conflicts over formally allocated resources are most easily resolved when all resources are allocated to the innovation initiative through a single document and a single process.

6. Interpersonal persuasion is often insufficient to get the Shared Staff to give enough time and energy to the innovation initiative. Stronger incentives and additional resources are frequently necessary.

7. Maintaining a healthy partnership is difficult because the two units are quite different and unlikely to naturally work well together.

Run a Disciplined Experiment

I N PART II, THE NEXT THREE CHAPTERS, we will describe how to *plan* an innovation initiative and how to *evaluate* its progress. Innovation initiatives require a far different approach from that of ongoing operations, and most companies inadequately distinguish between the two.

In managing their ongoing operations, companies strive for performance discipline. For innovation initiatives, however, they ought to strive for discipline of a different form: disciplined experimentation. Indeed, all innovation initiatives, regardless of size, duration, or purpose, are projects with uncertain outcomes. They are experiments.

As innovation leader, one of your critical managerial responsibilities is to learn as the initiative proceeds. If there is a substantial sum of money at stake, the sooner the learning, the better. Initial plans for innovation initiatives are typically riddled with guesswork. As a result, the competitor that wins is rarely the one with the best initial plan; it is the one that learns the fastest.

But drawing the right lessons learned from an experiment-in-progress is hard. It requires discipline. In the next three chapters, we examine best practices for following a rigorous learning process. There are three steps:

1. *Formalize the experiment.* The basic principles for learning from experiments are familiar but hard to follow.

2. *Break down the hypothesis.* All but the simplest innovation initiatives are really compound experiments. There are two or more uncertain conjectures.

3. *Seek the truth.* Myriad pressures in organizations push people toward interpretations of results that are comfortable and convenient rather than analytical and dispassionate. These pressures must be understood and overcome.

CHAPTER FOUR

Formalize the Experiment

IN 2004, SONY CORPORATION'S electronics business in the United States suffered when the press took note of its poor customer service. Two years later, the company was earning rave reviews instead. At the heart of its approach to improvement was a series of disciplined experiments.

Sony asked one of its senior executives, Phil Petescia, to review the company's customer service practices. Petescia hypothesized that customer service agents would be more effective if they specialized in certain products or certain issues. He anticipated that they would develop deeper knowledge and solve more problems. And he guessed that when agents became more successful, they would feel more satisfied and work harder. Success would beget more success.

The biggest challenge with such an approach was connecting each call to the right specialist on the first try. Customers lost patience when an agent failed to solve their problem and then connected them to a new agent. To address the challenge, Sony employed a familiar technology, an automated system to ask customers diagnostic questions. This had to be done cautiously, however. Customers became agitated when a machine asked too many questions.

To discover the best possible approach, Petescia ran experiments. He varied both the number of questions and the questions asked. By doing so, he discovered where customers hit their "point of pain" when interacting with a computer. He also was able to zero in on diagnostic questions that customers had trouble with and eliminate them. For example, customers had trouble accurately assessing whether they had a software problem or a hardware problem.

Petescia and his team took a formal approach to experimenting. With every change, they carefully tracked and analyzed whether the call reached the right specialist on the first try, whether the customer reported that the problem was resolved, and whether the customer was satisfied with the experience. With each trial, Sony learned. Its dramatic improvement shows the power of disciplined experimentation.

Trying something experimental is easy. Learning from the experiment is not. We start this chapter by defining exactly what learning is and showing why it is so hard. We then give a brief overview of the key steps in a process for disciplined experimentation.

Then we explain ten specific principles for disciplined experimentation. As we will show, each of these principles sharply diverges from standard practices for ongoing operations. These differences are exactly what make learning from experiments difficult in a business context. We will conclude the chapter with several examples of companies that have succeeded by taking a formal approach to running experiments.

How Learning Leads to Results

When we speak with executives about the overriding importance of learning from experiments, we sometimes sense a degree of impatience. The overwhelming goal, in the minds of some, is not *learning*; it is *results*. Learning is a soft and squishy objective; results, on the other hand, are what business is all about.

We sympathize with that point of view. Learning, as an outcome, can sound like a consolation prize. "Sorry that the project failed, boss, but, let me tell you, we learned a *ton*." We get it. With innovation, however, placing primary focus on learning rather than results actually leads to better results.

We are not talking about learning in a general, feel-good sense. We are talking about a very specific type of learning. For our purposes, learning is the process of turning speculative predictions into reliable predictions.

Companies launch innovation initiatives when predicted outcomes justify the investment. But these predictions are based on assumptions. They are guesses. In some cases, they are wild guesses. As you learn, you convert assumptions into knowledge. Wild guesses become informed estimates, and informed estimates become reliable forecasts. (See figure 4-1.) The best indicator that you are learning is that your predictions get better.

FIGURE 4-1

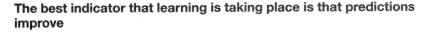

The best indicator that learning is taking place is that predictions improve

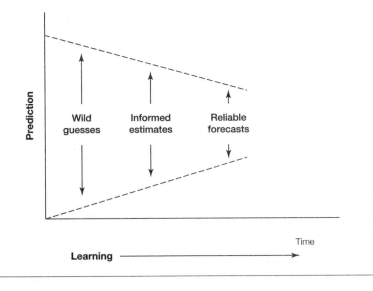

To see how learning leads to results, consider two companies that invest in the same innovation initiative. Both have identical plans. The odds of success are roughly one in three. The first company maintains a traditional focus on results. The second, instead, focuses on learning.

In the first company, because there is no learning process in place, the leaders of the innovation initiative stick to the original plan—a plan composed at a time when there was little data, just guesses. When results start to fall short of predictions, the innovation leader becomes defensive. Knowing that the only acceptable outcome is success, the leader obfuscates unpleasant data and focuses on persuading decision makers to continue the investment, perhaps spinning a far-fetched story about how the initiative can still succeed. If the leader is convincing, the company continues to invest and continues down a road to eventual and expensive failure. Disastrous though this may be, it may not be the end of the story. The stinging aftermath of failure makes it unlikely that the company will retain the right lessons learned. Indeed, it may launch a second innovation initiative based on the same faulty premises.

In the second company, leaders of the initiative openly discuss results and question the original assumptions in the plan. As they learn, they update their predictions. When it becomes clear that the original assumptions were wrong and the original predictions are unrealistic, the company engages in a conversation about what to do next. Should it abandon the experiment? Alter the plan to change directions? Either way, it will achieve results that are better than the first company's. If the initiative fails, it will fail earlier and at lower cost. Or, if the second company sees a way to change directions to increase the odds of success, it might actually succeed. Each revision of the plan is based on more data and fewer assumptions. The picture gets clearer each time.

Learning is making better predictions, and the ability to make better predictions is imminently and immediately practical. When executives shy away from learning as a managerial objective in favor of being tough and demanding results, they are not being hard-nosed; they are just hardening the path to failure.

Some experiments *will* fail. That is inevitable. There is never any excuse, however, for not learning in a quick and disciplined fashion. Doing so minimizes the cost of failure and maximizes the probability of success.

Learning Cannot Be Left to Intuition Alone

We are all familiar, through daily experience, with the process of learning through experimentation. If you like to cook, you probably try experiments from time to time, changing ingredients or cooking methods, for example. Each time you try an experiment, at least implicitly, you make a prediction about how your food will improve. When dinner is served, you find out whether the prediction was right or wrong.

We will dedicate this and the next two chapters to describing a formal and rigorous process for learning from experiments. Yet, unless you are an unusual chef, you probably do not approach the experimentation process with any formality. You just do it, and with time and experience, you get better. Despite the informal approach, you probably learn quite readily People tend to approach video games the same way. Try and learn. It works.

It is important, however, to understand *why* learning comes easily in such situations. Cooking and video gaming represent rather idealized environments for experimentation because results are quick, clear, and complete.

Delays between actions and outcomes, even short delays, can wreak havoc on our ability to learn through experimentation. Have you ever stayed in an old hotel, one in which it took seemingly forever for hot water to make its way from the hot water tank way down in the basement to the shower in your room way up on the fifth floor? Can you recall how hard it was to adjust the temperature? You adjust the setting hotter. Nothing happens. You go further. Nothing happens. Further still, and then suddenly you are scalded. You start adjusting the other way, and again, and again, and then you are freezing once more. Delays between actions and outcomes make it much harder to establish intuitive connections between cause and effect.

Only a tiny subset of business experiments yield quick, clear, and complete results. Typical business experiments generate partial results, from time to time, along a lengthy journey from launch to fruition. Only by following a rigorous learning process will you efficiently convert these partial answers into a clear, aggregate picture.

In fact, large volumes of research demonstrate that when conditions are less than ideal, humans are exceptionally poor at learning through intuition alone. It becomes too hard to connect cause and effect. Biases interfere with good judgment.

Most of the innovation leaders we have spoken with are aware at some level that learning matters. Some even speak of taking an experiment-and-learn approach. Too many, however, leave learning to intuition. Most say the words *experiment and learn* casually, even with a shrug. They are aware, at least, that their project may not turn out as hoped. And they are committed, at least, to remaining open-minded about learning something from the experience.

But open-mindedness is insufficient. Intuition is flawed. Even when an experiment is easy to run, it can be hard to learn from. Lessons are not just magically acquired by those who are open to receiving them.

In fact, if you and your team meet to discuss lessons learned on the basis of intuition alone, you are likely to have a conversation that amounts to little more than an off-the-cuff exchange about the theoretical possibilities of what went right and what went wrong. Rather than dispassionately pursuing truth, you and your team will exchange convenient stories. In the end, the most gifted and persuasive storyteller will prevail.

The alternative is a rigorous learning process.

A Process for Learning from Experiments

The basic steps for learning from experiments are straightforward:

Before launching an experiment, write down what you plan to do, what you expect to happen, and why. Draw lessons learned by analyzing differences between what you thought would happen and what actually happened. Then, based on lessons learned, revise the plan. (See figure 4-2.)

That is the whole ball game! If you can execute this process rigorously and dispassionately, your chances of drawing the right lessons learned from a business experiment go up dramatically. The crucial learning step is the analysis of the disparities between predictions and outcomes. Through this analysis, assumptions are either validated or invalidated. Lessons are learned. Predictions improve.

This process has a formal name—the scientific method. For many, the phrase *scientific method* surfaces bad memories from youth. Perhaps the last time you thought about the scientific method you were studying high school chemistry, and maybe you didn't even like chemistry that much. Nonetheless, the scientific method is the innovator's indispensable friend. The process of learning through experimentation *is* the scientific method.

When running innovation initiatives, businesspeople need to behave more like scientists. We believe that disciplined experimentation should

FIGURE 4-2

Formalizing an experiment

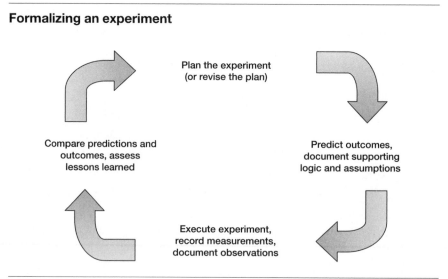

Plan the experiment
(or revise the plan)

Compare predictions and
outcomes, assess
lessons learned

Predict outcomes,
document supporting
logic and assumptions

Execute experiment,
record measurements,
document observations

take its place in the business school curriculum right alongside marketing and finance.

Each Project Needs Its Own Plan

With a basic process that is so easy to describe, what could possibly go wrong? Oh, if only the list were short. The learning process can break down in any number of ways.

Most of these breakdowns originate in an uncomfortable juxtaposition. For a scientist, formal experimentation is routine. For a businessperson, however, ongoing operations are routine and experiments are the exception. Many common disruptions in the learning process arise from awkward collisions between what's good for ongoing operations and what's good for experiments.

We've just given a basic description of a formal learning process. But business organizations already have such a process. It is, of course, the planning process. The basics are the same. As a part of routine planning, managers make predictions and later analyze the differences between predictions and outcomes.

Unfortunately, these high-level similarities mask fundamental differences. For example, plans for innovation initiatives have a much different purpose than plans for ongoing operations. A Performance Engine leader's central focus is to execute the plan. In an innovation initiative, however, the plan is a hypothesis. Your central focus should be testing and improving the hypothesis as quickly and efficiently as possible. Doing so leads to the best possible results. If your initiative is an entirely new business, your hypothesis is your strategy. Your job is not to execute the strategy, as it is in the Performance Engine, but to test and improve it.

This distinct purpose requires distinct thinking when analyzing results. The most fundamental premise underlying analysis in the Performance Engine is that a business is an ongoing concern; in other words, that past is precedent. This premise—that past is precedent—is the underpinning for accounting rules. Given that innovation is inherently new and uncertain—that there is no precedent—this recognition should make you squirm.

As a result, each innovation initiative must have its own, dedicated, separate, stand-alone plan. The stand-alone plan creates much-needed space for distinct thinking. It also prevents lessons learned from being obscured.

Innovation initiatives are small. Results may be not much more than a round-off error in the numbers for ongoing operations. Further, the Performance Engine's most heavily emphasized metrics often have little relevance to the innovation initiative.

A separate plan, however, is not a silver bullet. There must also be a different kind of process for creating and revising the plan. It must be a rigorous learning process. To create one, it is critical to recognize several specific attributes of the typical Performance Engine planning process that are anathema to learning.

The ten principles we discuss next guide formal experimentation and call out the necessary distinctions. Following some of the ten principles is straightforward. Others are easy to understand conceptually but more difficult to follow in practice, especially those initiatives that are larger, riskier, and more complex. In chapters 5 and 6, we offer several additional tools and techniques for staying on track.

Principle 1: Invest Heavily in Planning

When we launched the research that led to this book, we put together a budget. The first year, it took a long time to create that budget. We did not know how to estimate some of the activities we planned, and as a result, we made some assumptions that were not very accurate. Each year, however, our numbers got better. We spent less time on budgeting because we could draw on prior experience. As we zeroed in on our core activities, each year's budget looked more and more like the previous year's budget. We operated more and more like a Performance Engine.

Innovation initiatives tend to follow this same progression. At first, budgeting, planning, and predicting are all very hard. But, if the initiative succeeds, these activities steadily become easier.

Inside the Performance Engine, most activities are proven and routine. There are, of course, some variations from year to year, but planning is far from an act of *de novo* invention. As a result, managers become accustomed to working through the planning process relatively quickly. They may not anticipate the extra level of effort that is necessary to draft a plan for an innovation initiative.

Evaluating results is also more time consuming. When ongoing operations fall short of desired outcomes, the analysis is usually a process of identifying specific areas where performance fell short of standards—for example, "We fell short this quarter because our custom products sales force in the west region suffered three unexpected departures of senior and experienced salespeople." This type of analysis is relatively straightforward. Companies are accustomed to it.

Diagnosing why an innovation initiative fell short of expectations can be much trickier. Instead of comparing results to well-known standards of performance, the comparison is to a set of assumptions. The analysis is more abstract. There are often competing explanations of which assumptions were wrong and why. The analysis just takes longer to do well.

Unfortunately, for two reasons, the planning process for innovation initiatives usually gets *less* attention, not more. First, conventional wisdom dictates that as uncertainty rises, planning becomes less valuable. This notion rests on the belief that the value of a prediction lies in its accuracy. But that's just wrong. In fact, it entirely misses the purpose of predicting outcomes from experiments. The value of the prediction lies not in its accuracy but in its ability to serve as a benchmark for subsequent interpretation of results. The crucial learning step—the step at the heart of the scientific method—is analyzing disparities between predictions and outcomes. If you don't make clear predictions and document the logic underlying those predictions—a time-consuming process—you undermine this most important step.

Second, when executives who review plans divide their attention across the company, the natural instinct is to allocate time in proportion to size, that is, to give the most energy to the biggest divisions. But innovation initiatives tend to be very small. As plans are rolled up for more senior reviews, an innovation project can quickly get reduced to a single bullet point on a page labeled "initiatives." Rather than on the basis of the budget size, attention to innovation initiatives is best allocated on the basis of either the initiative's long-term potential or its short-term, bottom-line impact. A $10 million innovation initiative may not sound like much compared to a $1 billion business, but if the initiative fails completely, it alone chops a full percentage point off the profit margin.

Principle 2: Create the Plan and Scorecard from Scratch

In the Performance Engine, each year looks much like the previous year. This is convenient. It allows companies to specify standard cost categories, performance metrics, and planning templates to use year after year. It even enables the construction of IT systems that automate many of the tasks of planning, budgeting, and reporting.

With this added efficiency, unfortunately, comes rigidity. Innovation initiatives are deliberate departures from the past. They are rarely well served by standard planning processes, standard cost categories, or standard performance metrics. Forcing them into existing systems leads quickly to an emphasis on the wrong kinds of information and the wrong kinds of analysis. It also encourages managers to superimpose the well-understood model for ongoing operations onto the uncertain world of the innovation initiative.

To avoid this problem, planning documents should be customized. They should include new formats and templates for plans, budgets, and performance reports. It is best to start from a blank page.

Companies strive for efficiency in their planning processes as aggressively as they strive for efficiencies in any process. Therefore, this suggestion—to treat experiments as exceptions—will be met with resistance. But this step is critical. Yes, it is harder and takes longer. But without the extra effort, learning is unlikely.

Principle 3: Discuss Data and Assumptions

In our experience, businesspeople *love* data. They like to gather it, analyze it, present it, talk about it, and argue about its significance. When you present the plan for launching your innovation initiative, your CEO is going to want hard numbers, not just an anecdote about why the idea is promising. As Narayana Murthy, cofounder of Infosys, likes to tell his employees, "In God we trust. Everyone else must come with data."

We love data too. Performance Engine plans should indeed emphasize past experience, data, and detail. And, before making an investment in an innovation initiative, companies should absolutely collect as much data as they can to convince themselves that the investment is sensible and prudent.

But when it comes to innovation, talking about data is not enough. An overemphasis on data, in fact, can be counterproductive. Ongoing operations is a world of 90 percent data, 10 percent unknowns. A bold innovation initiative, on the other hand, might be just the reverse: 10 percent data and 90 percent unknowns. In such a situation, if all you can talk about is the data, then you are talking about only 10 percent of what matters.

You'd be much better off focusing on what you *don't* know by specifically delineating and discussing the assumptions underlying your predictions.

This is not typically what we observe. As a rule, businesspeople are infinitely more comfortable discussing data. First, data is just easier to talk about. The language is numerical and precise. Furthermore, when you have data by your side, it is hard to be wrong. There is comfort in data. There is truth in it. Saying, "I made that proposal on the basis of an extensive fact base," is reassuring. By contrast, as soon as you express an assumption, you open yourself to criticism. Acknowledging that "I had to make a bunch of assumptions" is rarely comfortable.

This is a discomfort that companies must overcome if they want to be successful at innovation. The assumptions are always there. The only question is whether or not you recognize them. And if you don't, you can't learn.

Principle 4: Document a Clear Hypothesis of Record

In ongoing operations, when it comes time to answer the question, "How did we execute compared to plan?" there are rarely arguments about what exactly the plan says. The plan is the plan. Most of the information in the plan is numerical and unambiguous.

Not so with innovation. The most critical information in the plan—the assumptions underlying the predictions—are often poorly communicated, poorly understood, and quickly forgotten. Fidelity between the plan as written and the plan as reviewed cannot be taken for granted.

Principle 3 advocated paying attention not just to data but also to assumptions when developing a plan. But it doesn't matter much if nobody can remember what the assumptions were when the results start to roll in.

Therefore, writing the assumptions down, as plainly as possible, is crucial. You must clearly document a hypothesis of record. When it is time to evaluate outcomes and assess lessons learned, each participant in the discussion must be able to return to this one-and-only hypothesis of record.

In the absence of this discipline, it is nearly impossible to have a productive conversation about lessons learned. If those involved in the discussion are just looking at numbers—the predictions and the outcomes but not the original assumptions—they will invent explanations of what is happening and why. They will likely invent new assumptions to support their stories, which undermines the learning process. The likelihood of any clear consensus about whether an assumption has been validated or invalidated goes way down. Biases and politics squeeze out learning. The larger and more complex the initiative, the greater the difficulty.

Principle 5: Find Ways to Spend a Little, Learn a Lot

In the Performance Engine, serving customers, defeating rivals, and maximizing profitability are the imperatives. For innovation initiatives, all these goals may be important, but learning—and learning quickly and inexpensively—is often the more immediate priority.

Thus, before launching a big experiment, ask, would a smaller experiment reveal the same information? Sometimes, the threat of a competitor getting to market first necessitates an immediate roll of the dice on a bigger initiative, but all else being equal, a slower, more methodical pace makes sense. This is the logic, for example, behind launching a new product in a test market before rolling it out nationally.

In addition, to ensure that you learn quickly and easily, take sensible steps to make it as easy as possible to interpret results. The ideal results are immediate and unambiguous. Therefore, consider: Are there any delays between actions and outcomes that can easily be eliminated? Is there any way to eliminate "noise" or unpredictable outside influences that may cloud results?

Finally, if the experiment you are running has multiple unknowns, it is worthwhile to discern in advance which of the unknowns are most critical. That is, which assumption, if wrong, would bring the entire initiative to an immediate halt? Is there any way to test this unknown first? With what measure?

Principle 6: Create a Separate Forum for Discussing Results

In ongoing operations, companies commonly review plans from multiple divisions, functions, or groups, in a single meeting. Doing so can facilitate the coordination of operations across organizational boundaries. It can help companies diffuse best practices. It can even help generate a healthy dose of internal competition.

However, meetings to review the results of innovation and ongoing operations should not be combined. Innovation initiatives deserve their own forum for discussion—a meeting that takes place in a different room, at a different time, and even with a substantially different group of people.

Reviewing innovation and ongoing operations in the same meeting is difficult because the nature of the conversation is so different. When reviewing ongoing operations, the baseline assumption is that the plan is mostly right. If results lag behind the plan, the conversation is about how to take immediate corrective action to get back to the plan. When reviewing an innovation initiative, by contrast, the baseline assumption is that the plan is probably wrong. If results lag behind the plan, the conversation is about which assumptions need to be revised and whether a major change in direction is appropriate. It is very difficult to work in both modes in the same meeting.

Furthermore, innovation initiatives are deliberate departures from ongoing operations. They are best assessed on the basis of distinct metrics and standards. When both innovation and ongoing operations are discussed in the same meeting, it is too easy to impose the criteria for evaluating the Performance Engine on the innovation initiative. We have seen this at several companies. Established metrics and standards of performance become second nature after they have been used for many years.

For example, at one company we studied, one that had a catalog with thousands of products for specific applications, the gross margin for each product served as a quick proxy for its overall performance. The cost structure for every product in the catalog was similar, and as a result, the gross margin standard worked well.

Confusion reigned, however, when the company launched a new general-purpose product that was made and sold in volumes several multiples higher than any other. As a result of the high volumes, sales, marketing, and development expenses were all much lower as a percentage of sales than historical norms. Even though the new product had an abysmal gross margin by company standards, its overall performance was strong. But the company almost pulled funding for the initiative because its low gross margins created the impression that the product was a failure.

Principle 7: Frequently Reassess the Plan

In your company's Performance Engine, it may be normal to discuss fundamental business assumptions after relatively long intervals, no more than once per year. But that is not nearly often enough for innovation initiatives.

You want to be sure to reevaluate your assumptions as often as new data is available that might validate them or call them into question. In a multiyear initiative, for example, you may need to meet to formally discuss fundamental assumptions once per month. Frequent reviews are important because the rate at which you learn is limited by the rate at which you review and revise the plan.

Principle 8: Analyze Trends

When evaluating ongoing operations, analysis is straightforward. Results either exceeded expectations or did not. The company either overperformed or underperformed. The quarter was either a success or a failure.

When evaluating an innovation initiative, the central question is not quite so black and white. The focus is not the *result* but the *trajectory*. Is the initiative on a path to success or failure?

Standard planning formats are not much help in assessing trajectories. They typically show aggregate data over a lengthy period of time, say, a quarter or a year. When reports are broken down into greater detail, breakdowns by customer segment, by product, by distribution channel, and by geographic region are all more common than week-to-week or month-to-month breakdowns. This makes sense for an ongoing concern, as there is not a lot of change within reporting periods. (Some businesses are highly seasonal and are the exception to the rule.)

In an innovation initiative, on the other hand, the objective is to create change. Innovation initiatives tend to be far more dynamic than the steady quarter-to-quarter sameness of ongoing operations. As such, reports totaled over long periods are of little utility. Change can easily be obscured or even completely overlooked. Trends are more meaningful than totals, because trends give both the result and the trajectory.

Perhaps you've seen two types of speedometers in cars. Some have a digital display; others, the more traditional analog (clock-face) display. While the digital display may make reading your exact speed easier, the traditional display gives both current speed and an immediate and intuitive sense of the trend—how quickly you are accelerating or decelerating. Analog instrumentation is better for innovation.

Principle 9: Allow Formal Revisions to Predictions

In the Performance Engine, performance expectations are rigid. Short of a crisis, executives frown on revisions to the plan.

Innovation initiatives are different. Early predictions are almost certainly wrong. Furthermore, by definition, the process of learning is a process of improving predictions. Therefore, if predictions are set in stone, learning is simply not possible.

This is not to say that as innovation leader you should feel free to make casual and convenient revisions to predictions. To the contrary, you should only revise predictions through a rigorous learning process. There must be an agreed-on lesson learned. That is, there must be new data that indicates that one of the assumptions in the plan is probably wrong. Only then can you revise the prediction and update the hypothesis of record.

Principle 10: Evaluate Innovation Leaders Subjectively

In most companies, leaders are evaluated primarily on the basis of the results they generate. This approach works very well for ongoing operations. There are clear standards of performance grounded in past precedent.

It does not work well for innovation. Holding innovation leaders accountable to plan has several toxic effects. Consider how you would behave if you knew that you were to be held accountable to plan. First, you'd probably lowball predictions. Of course, this goes on in the Performance Engine as well, but as there is more uncertainty in your innovation initiative, you'd have more room for maneuvering. You might also work hard to find the prediction that is just barely high enough to win funding. Or, if you can't get the initiative approved with numbers that you are confident in, you might just walk away from the effort altogether.

Now, think about how you'd behave once you've fallen behind the plan. You might withhold information. You wouldn't want to engage senior executives in a discussion about changes in direction because you'd fear that they would view a change in direction as an admission of failure. Instead you'd work harder and hope. You might even take unnecessary risks in the vain hope of getting back on plan.

But what if you were evaluated not on the numbers alone but on your ability to learn and adjust? When creating the plan, you'd expend your energies defining a clear hypothesis of record, not negotiating a low prediction. Later, you'd actively scan the environment for changes, you'd quickly share new information, and you'd *want* to engage your boss in conversations about changes in direction.

The more engagement, the better. The only way that your boss can evaluate you subjectively is if she is close enough to judge your behaviors and actions, not just your results.

_____

Table 4-1 summarizes the key differences between typical planning process for ongoing operations and a rigorous learning process.

We conclude the chapter with two examples of companies that have built formal approaches to learning from experimentation. The first focuses on new product launches, the second on new service launches.

Thomson Develops a Formal Process for Experimentation

Lawyers have a voracious appetite for information. For decades, Thomson Corporation served the legal community by publishing extensive volumes of case law (for additional background, see chapter 2). In 2000, seeking opportunities to serve its customers more broadly, the company intensively

TABLE 4-1

Key differences between typical planning processes for the Performance Engine and best practices for innovation

Planning principles for innovation	Norm in Performance Engine
1. Invest heavily in planning.	1. Invest in proportion to budget.
2. Create the plan and the scorecard from scratch.	2. Just modify last year's plan.
3. Discuss data *and* assumptions.	3. Focus on data.
4. Document a clear hypothesis of record.	4. Document clear expectations.
5. Find ways to spend a little, learn a lot.	5. Be on budget, on time, and on spec.
6. Create a separate forum for discussing results.	6. Separate forums are unnecessary.
7. Frequently reassess the plan.	7. Deliver the results in the plan.
8. Analyze trends.	8. Analyze totals.
9. Allow formal revisions to predictions.	9. Revisions frowned on.
10. Evaluate innovation leaders subjectively.	10. Evaluate based on results.

studied work processes in law firms, step by step and minute by minute. By doing so, the company saw many new opportunities to serve its customers.

For example, the company saw that in preparing to go to trial, attorneys study almost every aspect of past cases similar to their own. They gather a wide variety of legal documents, including briefs (documents penned by attorneys to summarize their arguments), pleadings, motions, memoranda, and court dockets. Getting these documents was cumbersome. Lawyers typically sent assistants to courthouses to dig through archives and make photocopies. If Thomson could provide an online database of such documents, they could make law firms much more efficient.

Thomson also identified several opportunities to develop software to make attorneys more productive. For example, litigators often needed to estimate the amount of money that might be awarded in a lawsuit in order to decide whether or not to take the case. To do this, they manually searched for similar cases and examined the judgments. Thomson visualized a software tool that would automate the process. And, because one of the worst nightmares for an attorney was missing a court date, the company conceptualized the possibility of creating an automatic software link between online court schedules and lawyers' personal calendars.

Thomson maintained a large product development group. However, most of the staff remained engaged in small projects, often individual efforts, to make improvements to the existing case law database. For example, many wrote annotations and created links between cases so young law associates could more easily research a chain of related precedents.

The product development group had no process for tackling the much larger development projects that the company was now visualizing. Rather than creating extensions to the existing planning process, the company took a critical step: it created a rigorous learning process just for the innovation initiatives. At first, the company dubbed the planning process the Big 5, referring to the first five major product development projects that the company invested in. Later, the name became Big X because the number of projects changed from one year to the next.

Thomson's Big X process exemplifies many of the principles outlined in this chapter. For example:

- *A heavy investment of time and energy.* The Big X projects involved only a small fraction of the product development team. Nonetheless, the chief executive of Thomson-West, Mike Wilens, took a direct and active role in shaping and overseeing the process. And, each Big X project plan was subjected to intense scrutiny across multiple functions.

- *Custom plans.* Each project had its own distinct plan that identified assumptions and methods for testing them.

- *Spend a little, learn a lot.* Many of the Big X projects were new document databases. Just gathering and digitizing the documents were costly. So, the company began offering data sets to customers well before the company had exhaustively collected every possible document. Once in the market, Thomson ran pricing experiments to zero in on the value that clients placed on the new product. Based on the price customers would pay, Thomson decided how complete a database to build.

- *Separate forums.* The Big X reviews were separate from reviews of ongoing operations or routine product development.

- *Frequent reviews.* To stay on top of trends in performance and to learn as quickly as possible, the team met for formal reviews nearly monthly, each time to discuss the fundamental assumptions in the plan.

- *Routine revisions to the plan.* The leaders of Big X projects had frequent opportunities to revise plans, but never made changes casually. They only modified plans based on specific new information and lessons learned, and with agreement from supervising executives. The finance group created a mechanism for adjusting plans and shifting resources between Big X projects at any time, depending on their trajectories.

- *Qualitative performance evaluations.* Thomson's senior executives observed innovation leaders closely, knowing that they could not be evaluated based on results alone. They tried to keep the pressure on, while at the same time encouraging learning and minimizing defensiveness when results fell short of expectations.

Infosys Crafts Its Planning Systems
to Support Learning

Ten years ago, Infosys was a small company with a giant ambition (for additional background on the company, see chapter 3). It intended to grow from a small provider of custom software applications for corporations to a full-service, end-to-end consulting firm. To do so, Infosys needed to launch and grow a wide range of new services.

Infosys's leaders were intent on learning as quickly as possible as these new service launches proceeded. As such, the company treated the planning process differently for these initiatives.

Several elements of its approach are noteworthy. For example, the company:

- *Viewed innovation as disciplined experimentation.* Infosys recognized the uncertainty associated with its new service launches and regarded the planning cycle as a learning loop.

- *Created plans and scorecards from scratch.* For some new service launches, the company created separate software and systems to support the planning process. This ensured that the metrics and expectations built into the software and systems for the core business did not get superimposed on the new service. Instead, the company rethought each scorecard from scratch. For example, when the company launched a new service to take over ongoing operations of mission-critical IT systems for clients, system downtime became a crucial new measure.

- *Shifted attention from data to assumptions.* In reviews, Infosys focused discussions on assumptions, specifically, on conjectures about relationships between actions and outcomes. To ensure that discussions did not get bogged down in discussions about the accuracy of performance data, the company resolved all potential data issues in advance of the meeting.

- *Spent a little, learned a lot.* Infosys identified the most critical unknowns and metrics for resolving them. For example, when launching a new software testing service, Infosys invested heavily in tools to automate the testing process. But to what extent could the testing process be automated? Infosys tracked "fraction of testing automated" to find out.

- *Monitored trends.* The company learned that an upward trend in a new service's revenue productivity (revenue per employee) was an early indicator that the new service was on a trajectory to success.

- *Allowed formal revisions to plans.* In its core business, Infosys expected very high levels of predictability. The company measured the quality of its forecasts and, by its own calculation, achieved 92 percent accuracy. For new service launches, however, the company accepted even 50 percent accuracy. (What if you have a new service with only three clients and one of them cancels?) As service launches proceeded and Infosys learned more, it revised plans. Over time, the company ratcheted up its expectations for forecast accuracy.

- *Evaluated innovation leaders qualitatively.* Infosys's CEO, Nandan Nilekani, went out of his way to give innovation leaders his support. In particular, he recognized that innovation leaders could not be held to Performance Engine standards. They had to be evaluated based on actions, behaviors, decision making, and learning, and that required closer involvement and observation.

Formalizing the Experiment: Observations and Recommendations

1. Innovation leaders should consider learning quickly a top objective. Quick learning leads directly to better results.

2. Learning cannot be left to intuition. The alternative is a rigorous learning process based on the scientific method.

3. Learning is a process of turning speculative predictions into reliable predictions.

4. Each innovation initiative requires its own dedicated, separate, stand-alone plan.

5. Invest heavily in planning and evaluating innovation initiatives, out of proportion to the resources they consume.

6. Write a custom plan for each initiative, with custom metrics and cost categories.

7. Discuss assumptions. Do not get as absorbed in discussing data as you would in the Performance Engine. Innovation is a world in which there are far more unknowns than knowns.

8. Document a single, clear, hypothesis of record for each innovation initiative. Ensure that the team can recall the same assumptions many weeks later, when it is time to interpret results.

9. Try to spend a little, learn a lot.

10. Discuss results from innovation initiatives in dedicated forums, outside meetings held to analyze and discuss results from ongoing operations.

11. Review innovation initiatives frequently. The rate at which you learn is directly tied to the frequency at which you review and reassess the plan.

12. Assess whether innovation initiatives are on a trajectory to success by monitoring trends in performance.

13. Predictions must be revised as lessons are learned—that is, when data suggests that an assumption was probably wrong. Plans should never be revised casually.

14. Innovation leaders must be evaluated subjectively. Doing so requires close observation. The results do *not* speak for themselves.

CHAPTER FIVE

Break Down the Hypothesis

C HANCES ARE YOU THINK you are a better-than-average driver. Almost everyone does. And for that reason, you probably think that auto insurance is fundamentally unfair. You send in your premium each month, and where does the money go? It pays for the mistakes of all the other drivers—the *bad* drivers. Making matters worse, when you have your one-and-only accident, your insurance company punishes you by raising your rates.

Sharp customer dissatisfaction is a wide-open door for an innovator. Yet this particular door remained open for decades, perhaps due to the dominance of risk management professionals in the insurance industry and the corresponding lack of empowerment of experts in consumer behavior.

One company in which this balance of power has shifted is Allstate. Roger Parker, the company's vice president of marketing and innovation, redefined the innovation process to ensure that the voice of the customer was stronger throughout.

One of the fruits of Parker's labors was Your Choice Auto (YCA), a new product Allstate designed to address consumers' core frustrations with auto insurance. YCA included such features as accident forgiveness, which guaranteed no increase in premiums following an accident, and cash rewards for accident-free driving. There were several YCA packages that offered various levels of rewards and forgiveness.

When it came time to take YCA to market, Parker's team vigorously debated the best way for agents to explain and sell YCA to customers. All agreed that salespeople should first emphasize rewards for good driving and forgiveness for accidents. Beyond this start, there were advocates for at least five different approaches: (1) explain all options and let the customer choose, (2) work with customers to diagnose what was best for them, (3) offer the option priced just below what the customer was currently paying and explain the others if needed, (4) start with the lowest-priced package and then sell up if possible, or (5) start with the highest-priced package and work down until the sale was made.

To determine the winning approach, Allstate tested the options as scientifically as possible. It paid its agents to try each approach and to track the outcomes. It set up a special Web site to collect data on hundreds of agent-customer interactions.

The results stunned the team. The last approach, starting with the highest-priced package, was the approach with the least support in advance of the test. It was also the winner by a large margin.

With the winning sales approach in hand, Allstate launched YCA in one state. The outcome: YCA was an unambiguous success. Allstate quickly expanded the offering and spread similar concepts to other categories such as homeowner's insurance. By 2007, YCA was available in nearly all fifty states.

From One Unknown to Many

Allstate's disciplined experiment-and-learn approach resolved the unknown that Parker was most concerned with—how best to sell YCA. But there were many other unknowns. Which of YCA's features would have the greatest appeal to customers? How much would they be willing to pay for each? Would Allstate really be able to persuade agents to overcome years of practice talking about coverage limits and deductibles and sell in a new way? Critical to Allstate's risk analysts, would YCA tend to attract safer or more dangerous drivers? And, of course, would the product be profitable?

Simple initiatives, say, to improve the efficiency of a process, often have just one unknown. Game-changing innovations like YCA, however, have several. That makes the learning challenge more complex. It becomes crucial to break down the hypothesis from an aggregate conjecture, such as "YCA can generate profitable growth," to the smaller assumptions that the larger goal depends on, such as "YCA will attract safer drivers."

In the best case, each unknown can be isolated and separately tested in laboratory-like conditions, the way Allstate determined the best sales approach for YCA. The more common situation, however, is that the unknowns are interrelated and can be resolved only by actually launching the initiative.

Had YCA proven to be something other than an unambiguous success, Allstate would have been presented with a much more complex learning challenge. It would have needed to assess which of several possible assumptions was wrong and what specific change in direction was appropriate.

We have seen that companies struggle with such complexity. At the core of the problem, typically, is the lack of a crucial foundation for any conversation about the best interpretation of results: a clear and shared hypothesis of record.

Creating a hypothesis of record is difficult. Teams are composed of specialists. Each tends to have a distinct point of view, grounded primarily in his or her area of expertise. To get to a clear and shared hypothesis of record, each must articulate his or her assumptions. Then, the team must bring all perspectives together, reconcile any conflicting assumptions, and create a single hypothesis that is formally tested.

Our aim in this chapter is to offer a few simple tools and techniques for building a shared hypothesis of record to guide the learning process. Doing so makes it much easier to follow several of the principles outlined in chapter 4, including documenting a clear hypothesis of record, taking more time to talk about assumptions and less time to talk about data, spending a little while learning a lot, and focusing on trends, not totals.

Better Conversations, Not Better Spreadsheets

The key to dealing with complexity is to focus on having good conversations about assumptions. This is counterintuitive. Many companies try to deal with complexity with analytical firepower and sophisticated mathematics. That is unfortunate, since the most essential elements of the hypothesis of record can typically be communicated through simple pencil-and-paper sketches. A good learning conversation is qualitative. It is about assumptions, not numbers.

The tools we offer in this chapter support conversational modeling, rather than mathematical modeling. Conversational models enable a group to quickly engage in a discussion about whether an innovation initiative is succeeding or failing, why, and what to do about it.

You may intuitively connect rigor with quantification. The connection is natural. However, learning from experiments requires more process discipline than analytical discipline. We have seen that there is much more leverage in improving conversations than there is in improving analysis.

To be clear, we are not arguing *against* quantification. Even when calculations are just estimates, a spreadsheet model demonstrates that there is at least a plausible argument that an initiative will earn a healthy return.

In addition, a good spreadsheet model enhances the conversational model. The analyst's job is to build a spreadsheet model that is entirely consistent with the assumptions in the conversational model and then seek additional insights only possible through calculation. Sometimes quantifying the model will show the nonintuitive implications of certain combinations of assumptions. Sometimes it will help refine the assessment of results. Sometimes it will lead to more accurate predictions.

But spreadsheets have a crucial weakness. A spreadsheet is an exceptionally poor tool for documenting and sharing the hypothesis of record. When you open a spreadsheet file, what you see are numbers, not assumptions. The thinking underlying the calculations is what matters most, but it is buried in equations that are difficult to review and interpret.

Think about it. When someone else builds even a modestly complex spreadsheet and sends it to you with no explanation and no documentation, you have to work hard to get inside the head of the spreadsheet builder and understand his logic and his assumptions. People often have this frustration even with their own spreadsheets. You may be familiar with this experience: You build a spreadsheet and put a great deal of effort into it. It is really good. You set it aside. A few months later, you need to revisit it. You open the file and start working. But soon you realize that you have no idea what you were thinking when you built the spreadsheet. You spend hours trying to refresh your memory, reviewing dozens of equations, cell by cell. By the time you are done, you might as well have just built the spreadsheet from scratch a second time.

Too often, we see extraordinary efforts to build the perfect spreadsheet to prove the case for investment. We'd like to shift much of the effort that goes into perfecting spreadsheet models to improving conversations about the underlying assumptions.

As part of our work, we have created a simulation-based exercise in which small teams manage a new business launch. In their first attempt, results are very poor. But then we introduce techniques for conversational modeling and run the simulation again. Inevitably there are complaints about having too little time to develop a quantitative plan. We disallow spreadsheets and discourage anything more than back-of-the-envelope math. Nonetheless, the results are inevitably *much* better in the second run.

That's the power of getting a team engaged in talking about what matters most. What is the hypothesis of record that we are testing? What are the specific assumptions? What evidence is there to suggest that these assumptions are either valid or invalid?

What Are We Spending Money On? Why?

A hypothesis of record, at its core, is a conjecture about cause and effect that connects planned actions to desired outcomes. It tells an "if–then" success story: if we take a certain action, then we will get a desired result. Since the actions generally involve spending money, the hypothesis of record, first and foremost, addresses two commonsense questions: What are we spending money on? Why?

Diagramming assumptions about actions and outcomes is straightforward. The cause-and-effect diagram in figure 5-1 suggests that action A will have an impact on outcome B. Innovation hypotheses often take the form of a single action leading to a *sequence* of outcomes. Action A will have an impact on outcome B, which will have a subsequent impact on outcome C.

For example, one medical device manufacturer we spoke with believed that its new product would succeed only if it was adopted by opinion leaders who had specific needs. The manufacturer's conjecture was that if it invested in features to meet these needs (action A), the opinion leaders would purchase the product (outcome B), and then they would recommend the product to many others (subsequent outcome C).

The most common mistake that people make when using this diagramming technique is to start mapping a sequence of actions instead of mapping cause-and-effect relationships. In other words, they create maps that indicate "First, we'll take action A, then action B, then action C" instead of "We anticipate that action A will lead to outcome B and then to subsequent outcome C." Actions should show up *only* at the bottom of each chain.

FIGURE 5-1

Mapping cause-and-effect

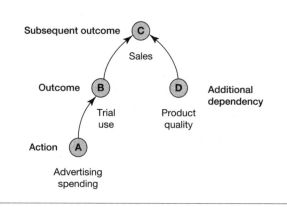

This technique can be used to create almost any hypothesis of record. We have found the following sequence of steps usually works well:

1. Divide the budget for the innovation initiative into a small number of spending categories, say, five or fewer.

2. For each category, sketch a sequence of outcomes and subsequent outcomes. Try to end each chain with a financial outcome such as revenues.

3. If possible, choose outcomes that are specific, unambiguous, and measurable. However, do not exclude a critical part of your hypothesis just because it is not easily measurable.

4. Identify additional factors that each outcome depends on. For example, consider a conjecture that advertising spending will lead to trial use of a new product, and trial use will lead to sales. The connection between trial use and sales is also dependent on product quality. Again, see figure 5-1.

5. Once you have a cause-and-effect chain for each spending category, look for overlaps. For example, multiple chains likely end with revenues. Create a single cause-and-effect map with no duplicate outcomes. This integrated diagram is the backbone of the conversational model. It tells the story of what you are spending money on and why.

6. Consider also adding critical nonspending decisions, such as price, and competitor actions, such as the competitor's marketing spending. Show how these actions could have an impact on the outcomes already on the diagram.

7. Keep it simple. A usable diagram fits on one page. It has no more than about twenty outcomes. Any more complex than that, and the diagram is no longer conversational. Reduce complexity by combining spending categories that are similar and by eliminating excessive detail in cause-and-effect chains. This final step is the hardest. Finding the right level of detail is a bit of an art. It takes practice.

These diagrams, simple though they may appear, are an effective way to help document and communicate assumptions about cause and effect. With clearly documented assumptions, it becomes much easier, three months into an innovation initiative, for everyone involved to recollect the single, shared, hypothesis of record and quickly engage in conversations about which aspects of the hypothesis are accurate and which are inaccurate. The diagrams make it much more likely that there is continuity between the plan-as-written and the plan-as-reviewed as opposed to a drift of convenience from one hypothesis of the day to the next.

ADI Seeks a Solution for Cellular Phones

Looking for new opportunities of growth, Analog Devices, Inc. (ADI), a semiconductor company, entered the cellular telephone electronics market (see chapter 1 for additional background). During the ensuing years, ADI achieved mixed results, including some periods of success and some periods of frustration. Eventually, the company decided that it could only achieve consistent results if it grew to a minimum size that seemed out of reach. ADI decided to sell the business to MediaTek, a Taiwanese company that also saw the importance of scale.

At several points along its journey, ADI's thinking about how to succeed changed. Our purpose in sharing this example is simply to show how these changes can be crisply articulated through the use of cause-and-effect diagrams.

Phase 1: Achieve the Highest Sound Quality

The electronics package inside any cellular phone included at least three chips, one analog, one digital, and one radio frequency (RF) chip. Some major manufacturers of cellular phones designed and manufactured their own chips, while others outsourced electronics design entirely, looking to a company like ADI for a complete solution.

When ADI entered the market, cell phone users were often dissatisfied with sound quality, which heavily depended on the quality of the difficult-to-manufacture RF chip. ADI had world-class manufacturing skills and believed it had an opportunity to achieve a strong point of differentiation in the market through better sound quality. The company hired an expert in RF technology, Christian Kermarrec, who soon led the company's cellular handset division.

Thus, ADI's hypothesis in phase 1 was straightforward. It believed that a heavy investment in RF would make its product extremely attractive, and that would lead to sales—action, outcome, subsequent outcome. See figure 5-2.

Phase 2: Help Customers Win

ADI discovered that high sound quality was an important differentiator but not as powerful as hoped. After a couple of disappointing outcomes in negotiations with potential customers, ADI reevaluated its strategy.

Cellular handsets were evolving into devices that were far more functional than just telephones. They had begun their metamorphosis into

FIGURE 5-2

ADI's initial hypothesis

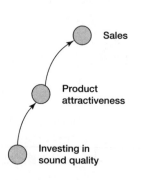

phones that are also small computers, Internet devices, music players, and cameras. Functionality was becoming more important than sound quality.

Therefore, ADI began investing heavily in the capabilities and the flexibility of its electronics package. It designed more capable digital chips and more sophisticated software and software development tools. It even named one of its chipsets a SoftFone to emphasize its flexibility and programmability.

In addition, the company invested more in the engineering support it offered during the sales process, working side by side with customers to create tailored solutions. Kermarrec's daily mantra shifted from *build the best chip* to *help customers win*. In fact, ADI wanted its customers to worry about little more than the final assembly of cellular handsets.

ADI's hypothesis had become more multidimensional, as shown in figure 5-3.

Phase 3: Ride Growth Waves in the Market

The strategy worked. In addition to many smaller customers, ADI won a major contract with one of the largest handset manufacturers in the world. The company was generating healthy profit margins, it was growing, and it had achieved a 10 percent share.

FIGURE 5-3

ADI's revised hypothesis

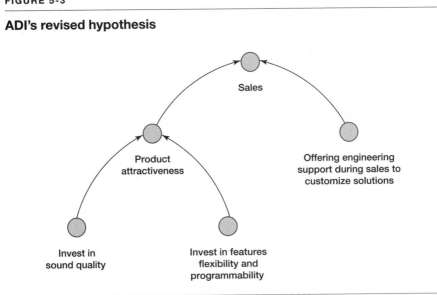

But ADI's fortunes were tied to its customers' fortunes. When its largest customer stumbled, it cut its orders to ADI by 75 percent in one quarter. Once again, the company reevaluated its hypothesis.

Kermarrec continued to believe that ADI's product was strong. The misfortune of one customer did not seem to suggest a need to fundamentally rethink the offering. The key, therefore, was to locate and capture the most rapidly growing segments in the market.

There seemed to be two critical possibilities. The first was in emerging economies, particularly China, where relatively new handset providers were poised for explosive growth. Kermarrec believed that ADI was in a particularly strong position to help these young companies build world-class phones much more quickly than they could on their own.

Second, Kermarrec believed that the cellular handset industry was likely to evolve in much the same way the PC industry had evolved. The major manufacturers of PCs, such as Dell, focus on efficiently selling, marketing, and distributing machines, not designing or manufacturing them. They rely heavily on partners for electronics design.

By contrast, many of the biggest cellular handset manufacturers outsourced design only for their lowest-end phones. But Kermarrec believed that the economies of scale in chip design and manufacture virtually guaranteed that this would change. He aimed to position ADI to win new outsourcing contracts from major handset manufacturers. The company monitored the attach rate, the fraction of handsets that were built with complete electronics packages from third parties. Figure 5-4 shows the revision in ADI's hypothesis.

Phase 4: Only Cost Matters

On the strength of its strong performance in China, ADI delivered solid results once again. But growth in China was not enough for ADI to declare victory. For that, Kermarrec's hypothesis about the evolution of the handset market would have to prove correct. The world's top-tier manufacturers would have to outsource design and manufacture of the electronics package for a much greater fraction of their handset models.

Unfortunately, this evolution in the market was happening slowly. And it was becoming clear that cost was driving the market more than any other factor. Many cellular network operators were giving consumers phones for free if they committed to two-year service contracts. As such,

FIGURE 5-4

ADI's hypothesis evolves

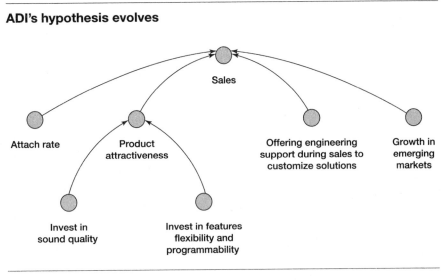

the network operators wanted to pay as little as possible for the handsets. While ADI's offerings were superior in quality, flexibility, and functionality, they were also more expensive.

There are heavy economies of scale in semiconductor manufacture. It was clear to CEO Jerry Fishman that lacking a major breakthrough contract with a huge handset manufacturer, ADI would never achieve the necessary cost position. No such contract came in 2007, and Fishman chose to exit the business. Figure 5-5 shows the reasoning.

Keeping Conversations on Track

Diagrams like those in the figures serve a critical purpose. They ground conversations about how an innovation initiative is progressing in a clear and shared hypothesis of record. Keeping conversations centered in this way is not easy. There are three forces to contend with.

First, on any given day, everyone involved in reviewing the business is immersed in immediate, short-term concerns. The most recently available data or the most recent, urgent customer problem can easily become the center of discussion. The cause-and-effect diagram helps elevate the discussion to strategic, long-term concerns, and places recent events in the context of the overall hypothesis that must be tested.

FIGURE 5-5

ADI's conclusion: Cost matters most

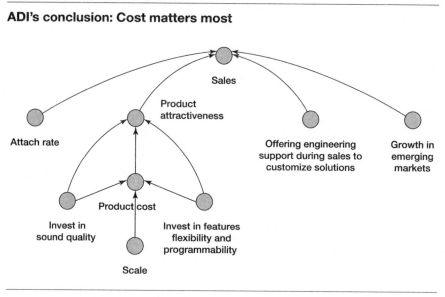

Second, discussions can easily become confused as people introduce alternate hypotheses or more complex hypotheses. The brief narrative about ADI tells only the most foundational and most dominant elements of its evolving hypothesis. But there were certainly competing theories and new ideas that emerged throughout the journey. A simple cause-and-effect diagram makes it much more likely that these competing theories will be made explicit. The diagram makes it much easier to say to a colleague, "It sounds like you have some new ideas about how we can succeed. Are you proposing that we alter our hypothesis of record?"

Third, there is a tremendous tendency in any established company to evaluate an innovation initiative based on criteria that make sense for the existing business but not for the innovation. Put another way, it is very easy to subconsciously substitute the (proven) hypothesis of the existing business for the (unproven) hypothesis of record. This happens, for example, when well-known metrics and standards from the existing business are applied to the new one, or when an argument begins with a statement such as, "We have always won when we have done A, B, and C." Frequent reference to the hypothesis of record can counter this natural tendency.

Innocuous as they may seem, cause-and-effect diagrams are powerful tools. They ground conversations in a single, shared hypothesis of record that evolves as an innovation initiative proceeds. They cost very little but have tremendous benefit.

Further Describing Cause and Effect

Cause-and-effect relationships are the most essential elements of a hypothesis of record. For critical, controversial, or complex linkages, however, you should take the time to discuss and document additional details about the cause-and-effect relationship.

Specifically, you can describe how much an outcome may change and how long it will take. A cause-and-effect diagram will indicate, for example, that action A has an impact on outcome B. But how much B do you get for a certain amount of A? And do you get it immediately? In one month? In one year?

Simple annotations next to arrows on the cause-and-effect diagram can convey some basic ideas. For example, writing a plus or minus sign can indicate whether the relationship is direct or inverse. Words like *proportional* or *exponential* convey a sense of how much, and brief phrases like *one-month delay* or *most benefit in first month* convey how long.

Graphs—simple line sketches—can convey additional detail. To describe "how much" as a graph, put the cause on the *x*-axis and the effect on the *y*-axis. To convey "how long," put time on the *x*-axis and the effect on the *y*-axis.

These graphs need to be simple to be useful. Therefore, focus on just *one* cause-and-effect connection at a time, in isolation. Assume that all other factors remain constant.

Like cause-and-effect diagrams, these annotations and graphs are intended to be conversational, not quantitative. The general shape and direction of the curves on the graphs are important. Their accuracy is not. Axes on the graphs can be given rough and approximate labels, often including just a minimum and a maximum or a rough indication of the time frame, which can be conveyed with a simple label like "weeks" or "years."

From Hypothesis to Predictions

One way to test your hypothesis is to try to test each cause-and-effect link independently. Some cause-and-effect links can indeed be tested this way.

As best as possible, you create laboratory-like conditions and perform a controlled test in which nothing else is varied except the one cause-and-effect interaction you are testing. This is how, for example, Allstate sought the best sales approach for Your Choice Auto.

But testing each cause-and-effect link in a controlled manner is not always practical. Sometimes a link cannot possibly be isolated so that you can test the influence of just one action. In other cases, carefully testing each cause-and-effect relationship would slow you down so much that a competitor would beat you to market.

You have to do the best you can to learn under real-world conditions in which many actions and outcomes are changing simultaneously. Thus, you have to predict outcomes for the actual initiative, not just for hypothetically isolated cause-and-effect links.

Despite the complexity, the conversational approach is powerful. Mental simulation generates better predictions than most people imagine. You can make reasonable qualitative predictions through intuition and judgment alone, especially if you have first thought through each cause-and-effect link in isolation. The best format for predictions is once again a trend graph—time on the x-axis and an outcome on the y-axis.

Qualitative predictions are usually sufficient at early stages. The important questions are: Does the imagined cause-and-effect relationship exist? If so, are we seeing the effect at roughly the magnitude and over roughly the time frame we anticipated?

These questions can be resolved by qualitatively comparing predicted to actual trends. Spreadsheets just get in the way. The quantified business plan may estimate marketing expenses at 22 percent of sales, but early in the life of the initiative, the question is not whether 20 percent or 22 percent is the better estimate. It is whether or not there is any connection at all between marketing spending and sales revenues.

For example, the medical device company that we described earlier in this chapter hypothesized cause-and-effect connections between features targeted specifically at opinion leaders, sales to opinion leaders, and additional sales generated by referrals from opinion leaders. Learning whether or not these correlations exist does not require a complex mathematical model. Qualitative predictions of the trajectories for sales to opinion leaders and sales from referrals, followed by discussions about actual versus anticipated trends, will suffice.

Only after the cause-and-effect relationships have been validated should you shift emphasis to improving estimates of revenue and cost parameters and refining calculations of profitability and return on investment. In this later phase, quantification and mathematics become more important.

Build a Custom Scorecard

The process of documenting a hypothesis of record is also one of developing a custom scorecard. The most important measures for an innovation initiative are the ones that resolve assumptions—the ones that validate the cause-and-effect map.

It is not always easy to keep attention on the right metrics, however, because companies already have a scorecard in place. The most common performance measures likely appear on standard reporting templates, and they are likely an instinctive reference point for any conversation, formal or informal, about how the company is doing.

These metrics may or may not be relevant to the innovation initiative. One of the most common mistakes we have observed is the inappropriate application of Performance Engine metrics to innovation initiatives. This tendency quickly undermines the learning process. It creates confusion and leads to poor decision making.

At ABB, the innovative developer and manufacturer of electric power-generation equipment, Dinesh Paliwal, who led the R&D function, had a theory. He believed that the earlier the company involved customers in the R&D process, the more satisfied customers would be.

For decades, ABB prided itself on being smarter than the industry it served, that is, for knowing more about what customers needed than the customers themselves knew. The pride was not unjustified. According to Paliwal, ABB had created the first transformer, the first breaker, the first switch, and more. But Paliwal saw that ABB did not always fully appreciate a key difficulty that customers faced. Power-generation equipment lasts for decades. Sometimes the customer's greatest concern is the time, energy, and expense that will be required to get new machines working well with legacy equipment.

To test the hypothesis, Paliwal could not rely on ABB's standard reporting metrics. He created new ones. He measured the fraction of new product development projects in which customers were involved at the blueprint level and then measured how satisfied customers were with the process of installing new equipment. If both trended upward, it would validate the relationship between the two.

The example shows why every innovation initiative should have its own custom template for performance reporting. If your company has an automated performance reporting system, this likely means extra work creating a template and filling in the data manually each period. No matter. It is worth it.

There is usually some overlap between the innovation scorecard and the Performance Engine scorecard. For example, aggregate, bottom-line metrics such as return on investment likely appear on both.

But just because the metric is the same does not mean that the standard is the same. The benchmarks for good, fair, or poor results in the Performance Engine may have little relevance to the innovation initiative. On some metrics, results that look abysmal by Performance Engine standards may be offset by much better results on a different dimension of performance.

Imagine a manufacturing company for which the defect rate is a critical metric. This year, the company is launching a new product targeted at an entirely new customer segment. The defect rate on the new product will be measured, and it will be important, but it must be interpreted carefully. If the new product is more complex, defects may be higher. That may be OK, as long as other costs are lower, or pricing is higher, or asset intensity is lower, or customers are more accepting of defects.

Innovation initiatives are deliberate departures from the past. Therefore, you must make comparisons between Performance Engine results and innovation initiative results with extreme care.

Resolve Critical Unknowns First

One of the ten principles discussed in chapter 4 was to spend a little, learn a lot. To do so, you want to resolve the most critical unknowns first. To find them, work through the entire hypothesis of record, asking two questions about each cause-and-effect link. What is the likelihood that our conjecture about this cause-and-effect relationship is wrong? And, if it is wrong, what are the consequences?

FIGURE 5-6

Identifying the most critical unknowns

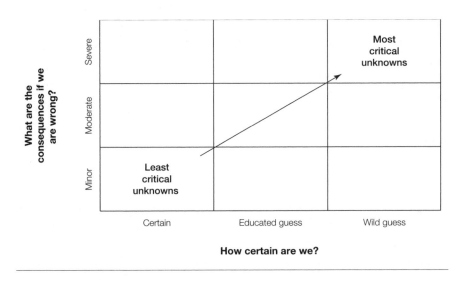

For most innovation initiatives, there will be a range of answers. Some of the links will be entirely speculative, while others are nearly certain based on experience in the established business. And the implications of being wrong could range from trivial to disastrous. You should regard those assumptions that are both highly uncertain and highly consequential as the most critical unknowns (see figure 5-6).

You should ensure that everyone involved in the initiative knows which are the most critical unknowns. They should be highlighted on cause-and-effect maps, and the metrics most useful in resolving them should be most prominent on the custom scorecard. When possible, you should test these unknowns first and at as little expense as possible.

One company that we studied, IBM, took a systematic approach to resolving critical unknowns early and inexpensively. In 1999, the company announced that it would endeavor to build the world's fastest computer.

The realm of supercomputing is far removed from everyday experience but of great importance to scientists in a few select fields. Molecular biologists, for example, need supercomputers to simulate the process of protein folding. Better understanding of the dynamics of protein construction in the human body will likely lead the search for medical therapies in new directions. Nodding to the great excitement in the biotech industry at the time, IBM named the planned computer Blue Gene.

At the time, advancements in supercomputing were reaching a practical limit. The machines were voracious consumers of electricity and, in the words of one IBM scientist, unless there were a fundamental design breakthrough, supercomputers would soon require dedicated power plants. Previous supercomputing advances had come in the form of better microprocessors, that is, better chips. Instead of continuing along that trajectory, IBM planned to use a thoroughly mundane chip, but it planned to use *thousands* of them, all linked together and working in concert. The concept, massively parallel computing, was new and uncertain terrain.

IBM was unsure whether it was possible to build such a machine, much less turn it into a profitable business. The most significant uncertainty was the relationship between the number of chips and the speed of the machine. IBM knew it would be nonlinear, but *how* nonlinear? At what point did adding more chips no longer result in higher speed? The chips needed to communicate with each other. But how much traffic would the network need to carry? And when would traffic jams start significantly degrading the speed of the machine? These questions could be resolved only by actually building prototypes.

As soon as it had designed a custom chip for Blue Gene, one that ran no faster than the typical laptop computer at that time, IBM ran a series of controlled experiments, starting with small and inexpensive tests. First, IBM built a Blue Gene prototype with only two chips. Then, the company doubled the number of chips, and doubled them again, from two to four to eight, and so forth. With each test, IBM learned more about the relationships among the number of chips, network traffic congestion, and overall speed.

Had Blue Gene run into a fundamental limitation at any point, IBM would have discovered the problem as soon as possible and at minimum cost. This is the essential logic of carefully identifying the most critical unknowns and testing them as early and inexpensively as possible.

With each doubling in the number of chips, the IBM team's anxiety rose. Success with a 512 chip machine surprised some of the network experts at IBM. How far could the machine go?

By 2004, IBM had built a sixty-four-thousand-chip Blue Gene. The speed limits imposed by the need for communication between chips were not as constraining as some at IBM had feared. Blue Gene was the fastest computer in the world. With the most critical assumption resolved—massively parallel computing had tremendous potential—IBM moved forward with the effort to commercialize Blue Gene.

Breaking Down the Hypothesis: Observations and Recommendations

1. Quick learning is most likely when there is a clear hypothesis of record that everyone involved in evaluating the initiative shares and uses as a frame of reference in any discussion of the initiative's progress.

2. Spreadsheet models have value. However, as a medium for communicating and documenting a hypothesis of record, spreadsheets are inferior to simple sketches of cause and effect.

3. A hypothesis of record is composed of a set of conjectures about cause-and-effect relationships between actions, outcomes, and subsequent outcomes.

4. The hypothesis of record can be further described by creating simple, qualitatively descriptive (not precisely quantified) graphs that address questions of how much and how long for each cause-and-effect relationship.

5. In the early stages of an innovation initiative, when validating cause-and-effect relationships, mental simulation of the hypothesis of record is an adequate approach to predicting outcomes. If predicted and actual trends are similar, the cause-and-effect relationship is validated.

6. Once cause and effect has been established, quantitative analysis becomes more valuable in refining estimates of the revenue and cost parameters that will shape profitability.

7. Never assume that metrics and standards used to evaluate the existing business have relevance for the innovation initiative.

8. After creating a cause-and-effect map, consider each linkage. How uncertain is each assumption? What are the consequences of being wrong? Identify the most critical unknowns, and find ways to resolve them quickly and inexpensively.

CHAPTER SIX

Seek the Truth

D O YOU THINK you'd enjoy constant pressure to innovate? If so, consider working in the toy industry. For Fisher-Price, the subsidiary of Mattel that focuses on infant and preschool lines, nearly three-fourths of annual sales come during the holiday season. Trying to anticipate what will sell in any given year can be migraine inducing even for the most experienced industry executives. Fisher-Price's head of research and development, Tina Zinter-Chahin, compares her industry to fashion: "Much the same, but with hard tooling."

To remain competitive, Fisher-Price produces several hundred new products each year. That puts tremendous pressure on the Fisher-Price team to come up with new ideas. The company relies both on the creativity of its product developers and on rigorous and formal observation of children and their parents playing with toys.

But Zinter-Chahin knows that innovation requires much more than just ideas. It requires that individuals in her organization take risks. Fisher-Price is currently addressing the fastest-growing segment of its market by adding more electronics, more software, and more content to its toys. As it does so, development costs rise and so does risk.

Willingness to take risks requires a sense of personal safety. Indeed, failed new product launches are commonplace in the toy industry. If Fisher-Price product developers equated a failed toy with a personal failure, few would stay in the job for very long. Instead, Zinter-Chahin is able to take great pride in her high employee-retention rates. She pays close attention to a routine internal survey to monitor how safe the product development team feels about taking risks and why. She also elevates lifelong learning to one of just four central cultural values for the team. And modeling the value herself, she benchmarks the team's overall approach to innovation against external organizations that she regards as world class.

In addition, she has achieved a sense of psychological safety in risk taking through small everyday actions. For example, in team sessions focused on creative idea development, she ensures that conversations always start with the positive points of an idea, even if there are numerous flaws in it.

The most emotionally charged moments, however, do not come while seeking great ideas. They come about six weeks after launch—at the Moment of Truth. By that time, it is clear to Fisher-Price whether or not a new product is a winner or a loser. At these Moments of Truth, Zinter-Chahin's actions have the greatest potential to either strengthen or damage the team's sense of safety.

For the winners, the team applauds and celebrates. And for the losers? Zinter-Chahin avoids penalizing product development leaders unless their *effort* was lacking. Instead, she focuses on lessons learned. What can the organization as a whole learn? What can be applied to the next product development effort?

It is the right philosophy. But Zinter-Chahin acknowledges the difficulty of conversations to diagnose lessons learned from failed efforts, and rates such conversations among her team's bigger opportunities for improvement.

Many innovation leaders in other companies can relate. Conversations about failure are dicey. It is hard just to get them on the calendar. With all the pressures of the upcoming quarter, who has time for postmortems of the past quarter? And how much fun is a postmortem anyway?

Fun or not, these meetings deserve not just a slot on the calendar, but a great deal of energy and care. A failed innovation that generates clear lessons learned is a building block for the future. A failed innovation that is quickly forgotten is just a failure.

In a new toy launch, there is one most significant Moment of Truth. For most initiatives, however, there are many Moments of Truth along the journey from launch to ultimate success or ultimate failure. Each is more than just a learning opportunity; it is a critical chance to alter the trajectory of the initiative and to improve its odds of success.

The previous chapter discussed the mechanics of having good conversations about how an innovation initiative is progressing. This chapter is about how emotions and biases can undermine these conversations despite healthy mechanics. It is about Seeking the Truth at Moments of Truth.

Doing so is not too difficult when the innovation project is short and inexpensive. But as the stakes rise, so do the emotions and so does the difficulty of Seeking the Truth.

The conversations that you lead at the all-important Moments of Truth will determine whether or not you learn quickly. They are by far the most important step in a rigorous learning process. If you want to interpret results well, you must have an understanding of all the specific biases that can affect judgment.

There are seven biases. The first is by far the most common and the most dangerous. We will spend almost the entire chapter discussing it and its antidote. The remaining six are easier to understand, and the antidote is simply awareness that the biases exist and discipline in fighting them.

Bias 1: Overconfidence in Predictions

Think about what happens at Moments of Truth. You have new performance data that you can use to assess the progress of your initiative. In the subsequent conversation, you and your team address questions such as: Have we succeeded or have we failed? Are we at least on a trajectory to success? What is going well? What is going poorly?

The effort to find answers to these questions starts with a comparison between what was expected and what actually happened, that is, a comparison between predictions and outcomes. If there is a difference between the two, then the all-important question becomes, why?

Consider the more likely scenario, when outcomes fall short of predictions. (Innovation plans are usually optimistic.) The possible explanations are wide and varied, but any explanation can be put into one of two categories. Either the prediction was flawed or the execution fell short (see figure 6-1).

To maximize learning, the conversation should be dispassionate, analytical, and free of bias. But we have seen, in company after company, that there is an overwhelming bias in these conversations. Explanations in the latter category—those that support the general idea that execution fell short—are far more likely to be considered seriously.

FIGURE 6-1

Two kinds of answers to the question, "Why did we fall short of plan?"

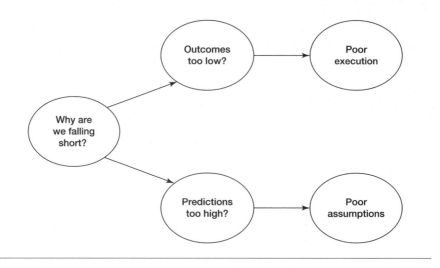

This bias is a devastating handicap in the learning process. Consider the extreme case, in which the only explanations considered fall in the category of poor execution. This implies that predictions are presumed correct! In such a circumstance, the probability of learning is reduced to exactly zero. To see why, recall that learning is a process of turning speculative predictions into reliable predictions. If predictions are, de facto, presumed correct from launch, then learning is, by definition, impossible.

The consequences are not just less learning but also drastically reduced odds of success in the innovation initiative. To presume that predictions are correct is to lock into the initial plan—the one made when actual data was at its minimum and guesswork was at its maximum. We think that the strong inclination to explain shortfalls as bad execution rather than bad predictions is both innovation's most omnipresent enemy and its most dangerous one.

Inside the Performance Engine, the Bias Is Healthy

This first bias has its roots in the Performance Engine, where it is deeply entrenched and rarely questioned. This is actually by design. The bias works in the Performance Engine because predictions can be made on the basis of a simple guiding assumption—that the future will look a lot like the past. Sure, the numbers change from year to year, but they change by a few percent and usually for well-understood reasons.

When the past is the precedent, predictions are accurate. When results fall short of predictions, it makes little sense to spend time contemplating whether the predictions were right or wrong. The only valid points of discussion are why the leader underperformed and what needs to be done about it. That is, in what way should the leader be held accountable for his underperformance? Perhaps he needs more attention from senior managers. Perhaps he needs some formal retraining. Perhaps he must be reassigned to a job he can handle. Or, perhaps the best solution is to encourage him to pursue a different career path at another company.

At many companies, the association between missing the numbers and negative consequences, between falling short and failing, is immediate and instinctive. Nothing is valued more than delivering the results you promise. If you do so consistently, you are promoted. If not, you may be fired. Everyone knows that these are the rules. Everyone lives by them. If a leader falls short and argues that expectations were unrealistic, he can expect to be dismissed as a weak excuse maker.

Some companies are well known for being aggressive about holding managers accountable for hitting the numbers in the plan, and they are usually high performers. GE is a good example. When we asked one young GE executive about the possibility of attributing a shortfall to factors beyond his control, he compared the tactic to throwing himself to the lions. At GE, if you miss your numbers once, you may be forgiven. If you miss twice . . . well, you were probably better suited for a different career all along. Such an unforgiving stance has worked for GE and for many other companies. In such organizations, your prediction is your pledge. It is your solemn promise.

Such an unwavering discipline of holding managers strictly accountable to plan can be extremely powerful. The specter of sharply negative consequences motivates. Leaders keep a close eye, week to week, on how the business is tracking against plan. When results fall short of expectations, they take immediate action.

But these positive benefits of a strong performance culture are available only in environments in which it is possible to make reliable predictions. The predictions that guide innovation initiatives, of course, are anything but reliable. This is the most critical difference between what is good for ongoing operations and what is good for innovation. In the Performance Engine, predictions may be presumed correct. For innovation, predictions must be presumed wrong.

In the Performance Engine, conversations should focus on bringing performance in line with well-known, well-understood standards. But in an innovation initiative, there are no well-known, well-understood standards. The objective is to discover what standards are realistic. The objective is to bring predictions in line with outcomes, not the other way around.

Getting Comfortable with Inaccurate Predictions

As leader of an innovation initiative, you must ensure that everyone involved, especially the members of the Dedicated Team and the supervising executive, is comfortable with the probability that the predictions in the plan are wrong. Achieving that level of comfort is difficult in any established company, and the stronger the performance culture, the more difficult it becomes.

For years, we have been speaking about how disciplined accountability to plan can undermine innovation. If there is one thing we have learned from these conversations, it is to approach them with great caution. Executives responsible for maintaining a strong performance culture sometimes react with knee-jerk negativism to any suggestion that innovation initiatives must be treated differently. Such comments play right into their greatest fear that if they give in to what innovators want, they will break the Performance Engine. Innovators, they fear, just want freedom. They want to hide behind uncertainty to avoid accountability. Allow it, and weakness will spread like a vicious plague. Discipline throughout the company will be undermined.

We get it, and we take any possibility of damage to the Performance Engine very seriously. And yet rigorous accountability to plan cannot possibly work for innovation. Therefore, innovation leaders must be evaluated differently from Performance Engine leaders.

To be fair, many of the companies that we have worked with understand this. They talk about the necessity of creating an environment more favorable for risk taking. They talk about changing the criteria for assessing the performance of innovation leaders.

But innovation leaders must trust that the change is real. Well-intended promises will have little effect inside a company in which managers make a visceral connection between falling short of plan and failing. When that visceral connection is strong, the likelihood of learning is near zero.

It is most critical that *you* are comfortable with the likelihood that the predictions in your plan are wrong. If you naturally connect falling short of plan and failing, whether due to the force of your company's culture or because of your own instinctive need to prove that your plan was right from the beginning, then what will happen if you do fall short? You will feel defensive. And defensiveness is toxic to learning.

When innovation leaders feel defensive, they stridently avoid revisions to the initial plan. They perceive revisions not as a positive sign of learning but as an admission of defeat. Defensive innovation leaders sometimes also undermine open and honest reviews with the boss by hiding or obfuscating unpleasant data. Or they take big, senseless risks in the vain hope of magically getting back on plan overnight. In other words, they will do anything but Seek Truth.

Searching for a Solution

We've seen several approaches to dealing with the inherent fallibility of innovation plans. Some are better than others.

Perhaps the worst possible "solution" is to simply throw away the plan once the innovation initiative is approved. Given the uncertainties involved, writing an innovation plan can feel like writing a work of fiction. The predictions in them are wild guesses. Indeed, in many cases, those trying to sell the initiative have deliberately stretched the projections to make the return on investment look better. So it is not too hard to understand why innovation plans are sometimes perceived as having little or no value. Innovation leaders are often eager to ignore the plan, and senior executives sometimes enable it, either by establishing a grace period in which missing the plan is understandable or by setting only broad parameters for acceptable performance, such as, "Just don't damage the brand," or "Prove you are on a trajectory to profitability within two years."

An assumption underlying this "solution" is that the value of a plan lies in its accuracy. But that is wrong. The value of an innovation plan is that it serves as a benchmark for subsequent learning. A rigorous learning process is one of improving predictions by improving the hypothesis of record. Throw away the plan, and you throw away the hypothesis. You and your supervising executive are mutually responsible for staying engaged in reviewing and revising the plan. To ignore the plan is to leave learning to intuition alone.

We have seen better solutions at several companies. Infosys, for example, is a company with a strong tradition of accountability to plan. But it mixes other virtues into its culture that are conducive to innovation. Like Fisher-Price, the company celebrates lifelong learning, even choosing to grace the entrance to its corporate headquarters in Bangalore with a statue of the Hindu god of learning. And Infosys values humility, an important offset to the overconfidence that is common among innovation leaders. A dose of humility is necessary to acknowledge that initial innovation plans are usually wrong and therefore in need of frequent revision. As one Infosys executive put it, "If you are not humble, you cannot learn."

At Thomson Corporation, another company with a very strong performance discipline, we've observed several additional productive steps (see chapter 4 for more complete background on the company). For example, the CEO of one business unit, Mike Wilens, saw that the defensiveness and fear of failure that undermine learning only accompany downward revisions to the plan, not upward revisions. As such, Wilens learned not to push too hard for aggressive plans at launch. He saw that doing so could result in innovation leaders who wish to withdraw from or disown the plan ("Those weren't my numbers!"). Learning suffers, as does motivation.

So Wilens accommodated initial innovation plans that he knew were conservative. Then, in monthly reviews, whenever there was positive news, he pushed for upward revisions. Doing so gave innovation leaders a chance to win twice, once for hitting the original numbers and once for having the moxie to raise their ambitions. It was a clever approach, though not a complete solution, as it did not address how to handle (less frequent) downward revisions.

Also at Thomson, Wilens's colleague Brian Hall changed the way that he evaluated innovation leaders. There were two primary elements to Hall's approach. The first borrowed a page from Olympic sports like diving, where your score is based both on your execution and on the task's degree of difficulty. In Hall's view, leading innovation was always harder than leading ongoing operations.

Second, Hall understood that at Moments of Truth, you had to Seek Truth, and he evaluated innovation leaders on their ability to do so. In particular, Seeking Truth required surfacing and openly discussing all new information, whether positive or negative. As he put it, "You have to create an environment where it is comfortable for people to tell you openly that things are not going well. Most problems are not because people screwed up; they are because there is something happening that nobody anticipated. You have to let people know that you are going to support them and help them figure out how to respond."

Hall tried to create this environment through positive means, but he also created pressure through negative consequences. In his mind, there was a sin far worse than missing your numbers, one that could lead to a dismissal from the company. That sin was trying to hide information and spin a positive tale rather than to relentlessly Seek the Truth no matter where it led.

We admire the philosophy. Hall's method of holding innovation leaders accountable for behaving in ways consistent with the objective of Seeking Truth is a very strong one. Still, we think that even stronger steps can be taken to redefine accountability for innovation leaders.

A Framework for Accountability

Many executives fear weakening performance discipline by giving special treatment to innovation leaders. The fear would not be so great if they understood that the alternative to accountability to plan is not chaos. The alternative is a different form of accountability, one that is equally disciplined and rigorous.

Indeed, there are three distinct modes of accountability. Leaders can be held accountable for results, for actions, or for learning. Each is defined by its own central evaluation criterion, as shown in the list.

Type of accountability	Focus of evaluation
Results	Did you deliver the predicted outcome?
Actions	Did you execute the plan well?
Learning	Did you follow a rigorous learning process?

Accountability for results is familiar, simple, and powerful. It is also very popular because the evaluation is unambiguous. As a result, people trust they will get a fair shake. There is no room for favoritism, no wiggle room, and no opportunity to fabricate excuses. Did you hit the numbers or didn't you? End of story. The unambiguous approach also makes it much more comfortable for the evaluator to give a negative review.

But strict, one-dimensional accountability for results is an effective choice only when predictions are reliable. The other two options, accountability for actions and accountability for learning, can be effective regardless of the accuracy of the predictions.

As an innovation leader, you should face mixed accountability. For predictable aspects of an initiative, you should be held accountable for results. For the remainder, you should be held accountable for actions or learning.

The sharp difference between the way Performance Engine leaders and innovation leaders are held accountable is the most important reason that we strongly advocate for separate forums for reviewing innovation initiatives and ongoing operations. It is too difficult to switch back and forth in a single discussion, and it is too hard to maintain a perception of fairness when both kinds of results are reviewed in the same room and at the same time.

Even with separate forums, a perception that innovation leaders are given special treatment can be damaging. Thus, senior executives must explain *why* it is reasonable for innovation initiatives to face different forms of accountability. In a nutshell, it is fair because the innovation initiative is not a bet that the innovation leader has chosen to take. It is a bet that the *company* has chosen to make. Therefore, the company owns the result. The innovation leader's responsibility is to execute the initiative well (be accountable for actions) and to adjust quickly as more information is gained (be accountable for learning). Put another way, the innovation leader's responsibility is to run a disciplined experiment.

You should negotiate a clear framework for accountability with the supervising executive before launching your initiative. It should be clear which mode of accountability applies to which metrics.

In the preceding chapter, we introduced a simple tool for mapping a cause-and-effect hypothesis. You can use the same tool as a guidepost for discussing accountabilities.

Each action-outcome linkage presents a choice. Consider a generic cause-and-effect chain between action A, outcome B, and subsequent outcomes C and D. Start with the A-B linkage and work up the chain. If there is precedent for outcome B, then you can be—in fact, you should volunteer to be—held accountable for the result. Then, working up the chain, as long as each subsequent outcome is reliably predictable, accountability for results is the right choice. This is the simplest form of accountability, and you should willingly embrace it wherever possible.

As you work up the cause-and-effect chain, however, you may run into a linkage for which the precedent is weak and the prediction unreliable. At that point, accountability for outcomes is no longer reasonable or effective. The mode of accountability must shift from results to learning. You should be evaluated not based on the result but based on your discipline in following a rigorous learning process.

Every cause-and-effect link beyond the first uncertain link is also uncertain. If outcome C is uncertain, so is outcome D. Therefore, once you shift to accountability for learning, you stick with it for the remainder of the chain.

Accountability for actions becomes important when *all* outcomes (B, C, and D) are uncertain. In addition to assessing the rigorous learning process, your boss should evaluate you based on this question: did you execute action A as well as you could have? Just as you should negotiate accountabilities with your boss in this way, you should do so with your team.

How You Should Be Held Accountable for Actions

Being held accountable for actions sounds less rigorous than being held accountable for results. But is it? If your evaluation is based strictly on results, your boss can give little thought to the evaluation until the numbers come in. On the other hand, if you are held accountable for actions, you are sure to operate under much greater scrutiny. How can your boss evaluate your actions if she does not watch very closely?

Though accountability for actions tends to be qualitative, actions are sometimes quantifiable. For example, consider an innovation initiative that involves selling a new product in an unfamiliar market. Holding your salespeople accountable for results would probably be unreasonable. It may be entirely reasonable, however, for you to hold them accountable for completing a certain number of sales calls per quarter and for documenting the lessons learned from each.

Or, consider an initiative that involves building a Web site. Traffic on the Web site may be difficult to predict, but you can still hold your team accountable for getting the Web site up and running on time and on budget, presuming that your company has built a similar Web site in the past. At Fisher-Price, sales of each new toy are hard to predict, but the product development team knows that it is on the hook to finish new projects within a few percent of budget, and it is well aware of the immovable nature of deadlines in advance of the holiday season.

Accountability for Actions Catalyzes Innovation at Deere

The benefit of shifting emphasis to accountability for actions can be seen even in small-scale innovation programs. For example, it was a critical element of Deere & Company's effort to build an effective process innovation program (for additional background on Deere, please see the introduction and chapter 1). The company, in partnership with its primary union, the United Auto Workers, began investing heavily in the program in the late 1990s, after it became clear that it would otherwise have to move more jobs abroad to remain competitive.

The program sought to motivate small teams on the factory floor to move forward with short projects to improve performance. The company and union found that gain-sharing bonuses for exceeding targets were powerful motivators. (To keep the pressure for improvements elevated, targets rose by a specified percentage each year.) But extra pay alone was insufficient. The company added many more elements to its motivational formula as it improved the program, including explicit goal setting, idea sharing across plants, and pride-building initiatives.

Even as the company saw that positive rewards were critical, however, it was also apparent that good old-fashioned accountability needed to be part of the mix. But the company's approach to accountability was not centered on results. The leadership team at Deere saw that a fair number of projects failed. Creating an environment in which too many teams were losers could undermine the entire program. Therefore, rather than criticizing a team for disappointing outcomes, the company took corrective measures only for a lack of action. Each work team had to document at least one improvement project per quarter in each of the four categories of productivity, quality, timeliness, and safety.

Deere is exceedingly pleased with results. Though continuous improvement was the number one topic on the agenda for two consecutive contract renegotiations with the union, it is no longer. It is just a way of life. Where outcomes are unpredictable, accountability for actions is a powerful alternative.

How You Should Be Held Accountable for Learning

Accountability to learning is the most challenging of the three modes. It is by far the most important for innovation.

You should be ready for your boss to hold you accountable by closely observing your planning process and specifically evaluating any of the following nine points. Failure at any one of the nine is a sign that the learning process has been, or is in danger of being, derailed.

Evaluation point 1: You are taking planning seriously. Innovation leaders have a natural tendency to disengage from planning, both because there are so many competing pressures for their time and because the inevitable guesswork involved in making predictions can make planning seem pointless. But without a structured process for making and revising a hypothesis of record, learning is unlikely.

Evaluation point 2: You have a clear hypothesis of record. A clear hypothesis is the backbone of the learning process. It should tell the story of what you are spending money on and why. It should illustrate what is known and what is unknown.

Every outcome included on the cause-and-effect map should be unambiguous and, wherever possible, directly measurable. For example, if the map includes market share, there should be clarity on the market definition. If the map includes product attractiveness, there should be clarity on how attractiveness will be assessed.

To assess the clarity of your thinking, the supervising executive should ask you probing questions about each cause-and-effect linkage in the hypothesis. For example, suppose the hypothesis includes a conjecture that face-to-face sales calls to physicians will drive sales. Possible probing questions include: (1) Why is this the hypothesis? (2) Are there alternatives to direct sales that we should also experiment with? (3) What do you think will be the hit rate for each sales call? (4) What do you anticipate will be the length of the sales cycle? (5) How much training and direct experience will salespeople need before they are fully effective?

Evaluation point 3: Everyone on the team understands the hypothesis of record. Learning is a team sport. The supervising executive can assess the extent to which the hypothesis of record has been effectively communicated throughout the team by routinely asking members of the team to express the hypothesis in their own words.

Achieving a clear, shared hypothesis at time of launch is important, but just a beginning. The hypothesis must live on. When it comes time to review progress, everyone must be able to recall it. This is not as easy as it sounds. Individuals involved in an innovation initiative learn every day, at least in an informal, intuitive way. As they do so, their mental models evolve.

When the team meets to review progress, step one is to review the hypothesis of record to get everyone back on the same page. This will be difficult if the hypothesis has not been carefully documented. Step two is to review results against the hypothesis of record and to make a formal choice about whether or not it needs to be revised.

Evaluation point 4: You are revising the hypothesis only when there is evidence to justify the change. Innovation leaders are often tempted to make revisions of convenience, often to reduce the pressure that they are under. The supervising executive should accept a revision, however, only when there is a good, evidence-based case for making it. Any downward revision should be accompanied by a reassessment of the likely return on investment and an explicit decision to either continue or discontinue the initiative.

Evaluation point 5: Everyone on the team recognizes the most critical unknowns. In order to learn quickly and inexpensively, you and your team must understand that not all assumptions are equal. Some are probably correct, while others are wild guesses. Some, if wrong, would compel a minor course change, while others, if wrong, would lead to a quick abandonment of the initiative. The most critical assumptions are the ones that are both highly uncertain and highly consequential.

You should have thought carefully about whether it is possible to resolve the most critical unknowns early and at minimal expense. However, the desire to minimize the cost of learning can lead to a methodical, sequential approach that is in conflict with the need to get to market quickly to preempt the competition. You should explicitly discuss this conflict with your boss.

Evaluation point 6: You and your team react quickly to new information. The rate at which you and your team learn is directly tied to the rate at which plans are reviewed. Therefore, your team needs to meet to review results much more frequently than is the norm in the Performance Engine. Monthly scheduled meetings are often appropriate, as are impromptu meetings to review unexpected new data. Also, you should improve your reaction time by using trend graphs as the routine format for performance reporting. That way, any change in your initiative's trajectory becomes apparent as soon as possible.

Evaluation point 7: You have a learning mind-set, and you are keeping your team in a learning mind-set. To win funding for your initiative, you will need to exude confidence and emphasize best-case scenarios. Once you have gained the commitment to launch, however, you must learn to bring a different mind-set into any conversation about how the initiative is progressing. In short, you must be humble enough to accept that the plan is probably wrong.

You must also help your team stay in this learning mind-set. A Performance Engine mind-set can easily reassert itself. Thus, be sure to use language that contributes to an atmosphere of scientific inquiry. For example, instead of "What will it take to get back on plan?" ask, "What evidence do we have that either supports or contradicts our original assumption?" or, "What is the simplest way to either confirm or deny that this cause-and-effect relationship exists?"

Evaluation point 8: You face the facts. Once innovation leaders invest their hearts, souls, and many late-night hours in an innovation initiative, it can become hard to see the truth, even when confronted with it directly. You must demonstrate an unflinching ability to openly discuss the performance data, even if it may lead to an abandonment of the initiative.

Evaluation point 9: Your predictions are getting better. The most concrete sign that you are learning is that your predictions are improving. Infosys puts forecast accuracy on the scorecard for its innovation initiatives. You should put it on yours.

Getting Incentives Right for Innovation Leaders

Many senior executives have shared with us their concerns about the proper incentives for innovation leaders. They believe, as we do, that leading an innovation initiative is a high-degree-of-difficulty challenge, and they want to attract the best people to the job.

That can be tough. Many high-potential executives avoid innovation. They worry that a failed effort may derail a carefully planned career. Their cautions are well founded. In too many companies, only results matter. A failed innovation *can* derail a career.

The key to creating the right kind of environment is to make two separate yes–no assessments. First, was the initiative a success? Then, did the leader do a good job? The latter is the more complicated assessment. As we have discussed, the leader must be evaluated based on mixed accountabilities for results, actions, and learning.

We think companies will do best when they offer a motivating menu of rewards (or lack thereof) in any of the four possible categories. Given our premises that the innovation initiative is the company's bet (albeit one that the leader probably encouraged and helped to shape) and that the leader's primary job is to run a disciplined experiment, we think the following choices are reasonable:

- *Initiative succeeds under good leadership.* The innovation leader earns a higher bonus than she could have received in the Performance Engine and also receives accelerated career advancement options.

- *Initiative succeeds despite poor leadership.* The company makes its best effort to move the innovation leader back to the Performance Engine without significant loss in career trajectory.

- *Initiative fails despite good leadership.* In this most important category, there must be at least a modestly positive outcome for the innovation leader. If the innovation leader is penalized, others will shy away from future innovation initiatives. Our recommendation: the innovation leader receives no unusual compensation or career advancement, but does receive a strong performance review and encouragement to lead more innovation initiatives. Furthermore, the company celebrates the failure and the lessons learned from it, and internally publicizes the company's desire to direct the leader to even higher-potential opportunities.

- *Innovation initiative fails under poor leadership.* Company assesses whether there is an opportunity for the innovation leader to move back into the Performance Engine but makes no promises.

Some may argue that companies should try to mimic the very high-powered incentives that exist in Silicon Valley so that they can attract the best people from the world of start-ups and venture capital. It is a reasonable argument. But in our view, Silicon Valley entrepreneurs are a different breed from the type of person who succeeds in leading innovation from within. In particular, start-up entrepreneurs have little experience in leveraging the full strengths of an established corporation.

Furthermore, very high-powered incentives, such as options on a tracking stock or a shadow stock, create challenging internal equity issues. They almost certainly create extreme tension with Performance Engine leaders, who will wonder why it is fair for the innovation leader to get rich by simply building upon the work that the Performance Engine has been doing for decades (nurturing a brand, customer relationships, and so on). And what about the Shared Staff members? Do they also benefit from stock-option compensation?

If you choose very high-powered incentives nonetheless, make sure that the downside risk matches the upside gain. If innovation leaders have the potential for explosive financial rewards, they should make the same sacrifices that start-up entrepreneurs make—zero to minimal salary, benefits, and job security.

The Six Remaining Biases

Even when there is a crystal-clear hypothesis, a rigorous learning process, and a rock-solid framework for accountability, bias is still a force to be reckoned with. We are, after all, humans, not Spock-like computation machines. You should be alert to the six remaining biases.

Bias 2: The ego bias. You will probably not be surprised to learn that we humans tend to attribute successful experiments to the actions planned and executed, and unsuccessful experiments to external influences—that is to say, bad luck. When judging whether or not evidence does indeed validate an assumption in the plan, it is always reasonable to ask, "How do we know we just haven't been lucky to date?" and "What might break this apparent cause-and-effect connection in the future?"

Bias 3: The recency bias. We are all prone to the error of focusing primarily on what just happened when forming conclusions, rather than considering the totality of what happened from the beginning of the experiment to the end. That is, if we are evaluating a one-year experiment at the end of the calendar year, what happened in December is likely to influence our thinking disproportionately. The best assurance of avoiding this pitfall is to ensure you use a wide-angle lens when reviewing results. Presenting outcome data as trend graphs dating back to the launch of the initiative is one of the easiest ways to create this mind-set.

Bias 4: The familiarity bias. This bias is the completely understandable instinct to gravitate to familiar explanations. For example, in an established, decades-old consumer products company, attributing market share gains to mass-media marketing spending might be natural, overlooking the alternative possibility that a newfangled Internet-based social networking initiative is what is really making the difference.

Bias 5: The size bias. Humans are predisposed to assuming that big outcomes are created by big actions. So, if your innovation initiative involved both a major capital investment and a simple process change, you would instinctively and quite possibly inaccurately attribute the bulk of any improvement in outcomes to the capital investment.

Bias 6: The simplicity bias. Assessing the progress of an innovation initiative can be complex and multidimensional. It is tempting to gravitate to quick-and-dirty explanations. The search for fast answers is particularly likely in informal, watercooler conversations, but those conversations can themselves influence more formal reviews by shaping people's entering assumptions. The most common quick-and-dirty assessment—and a dangerous one—is to simply apply a Performance Engine metric and standard to the innovation initiative. We have seen this happen despite the clear inappropriateness of applying the metric to the initiative. One consumer products manufacturer that distributed its products through retail had a standard for the maximum acceptable fraction of product returned. In assessing a struggling software initiative, the high rate of returns was a tempting fast answer for those who thought the initiative was a loser, even though standard terms of trade-in software gave retailers the right to return unsold items, not just defective ones.

Bias 7: The political bias. You will be competing with other executives in your company for resources, promotions, and prestige. In this competition, performance perceptions are powerful game pieces. Everyone whom you are competing with has a vested interest in making his or her own performance and prospects look as good as possible, while making yours look as bad as possible.

To do so, your internal competitors will seek simple but persuasive stories. They may quite intentionally try to influence perceptions of how your initiative is doing by reinforcing one or more of the previous biases. Someone might try to kill your initiative, for example, by highlighting anything negative that just happened rather than considering the longer-term trajectory of your project, or by finding a deeply entrenched Performance Engine metric and standard that reflects poorly on your initiative. Of course, you can also be guilty of political bias if you craft convenient explanations that have the opposite impact.

Seeking Truth: Observations and Recommendations

1. Objectively assessing the results from an innovation initiative is difficult. It is critical to be aware of the emotions and biases that can distort interpretations of progress.

2. The most common bias, and the most critical one to fight, is overcommitment to the original innovation plan. This bias is particularly prevalent in companies with strong performance cultures, in which falling short of the plan is equivalent to failure.

3. Innovation leaders should not be held strictly accountable for results. Instead, they should face mixed accountabilities—for results, actions, and learning—customized to the innovation plan and the nature of the uncertainties it faces.

4. Holding someone accountable for actions requires close observation of his work and, where possible, measurement of his effort.

5. Holding someone accountable for learning requires close observation of the planning process and evaluation of whether the experiment is being run in the most disciplined possible manner.

6. To attract the best leaders to innovation initiatives, companies must create the right mix of incentives. They must offer at least modestly positive rewards when initiatives fail despite good leadership.

7. The planning process for an innovation initiative is quite distinct from the planning process of the Performance Engine. It must be a rigorous learning process. It must emphasize hypotheses and assumptions, not data and precedents; it must question fundamental assumptions monthly or quarterly, not annually; it must present outcomes as trends, not aggregate totals for long time periods; and it must highlight custom metrics, not standard ones (drawn from chapters 4 through 6).

Moving On, Moving Up

I N THIS BOOK, we have described a model for executing *one* innovation initiative. At the model's foundation is a recognition that there are
fundamental incompatibilities between ongoing operations and innovation. While the Performance Engine seeks efficiency by making every task,
activity, and process repeatable and predictable, innovation is by nature
nonroutine and uncertain.

If you lead an innovation initiative, you must address the fundamental
incompatibilities by thinking differently about how you organize and how
you plan. You must build a team with a custom organizational model and
craft a plan that is only revised through a rigorous learning process. If you
do both, you'll fare much better.

And if you succeed, you'll move on and move up. You'll get promoted to
positions of greater authority in which you supervise an initiative, choose
the supervising executive for an initiative, oversee a family of related initiatives, and help shape a more innovative company from the top.

We conclude by extending the principles of this book to address each of
these challenges.

Supervise an Innovation Initiative

We studied a traditional chemicals company at an ideal moment, right at
the beginning of an innovation initiative—a major new biotechnology
business launch. The company was unusual. It spent several days working
through questions of organizing and planning for the about-to-be-launched
new unit.

We firmly believe that this was time well spent, although most companies don't have the patience for it. We understand. At launch, the team is eager to advance the technology, to build the product, to make the first sale. By comparison, worrying about organizing and planning seems, well, just a tad dull.

That is one of the major reasons why the role of supervising executive is so critical. When you take on the job, you must spend most of your energies on the matters discussed in this book—organizing and planning.

Several people have told us that our recommendations tend to fall into the category of "easy to understand but difficult to follow." That's right. They are difficult to follow because of competing instincts and pressures that arise in almost every established organization.

Therefore, as supervising executive, you must be actively involved. You must ensure that the innovation leader, the Dedicated Team, and the Shared Staff not only understand what to do but actually follow through.

Your responsibilities as the supervising executive fall into four categories. You must get the initiative off to a good start, monitor interactions with the Performance Engine, stay closely engaged in the rigorous learning process, and shape the initiative's endgame.

Get the Initiative Off to a Good Start

Amid the excitement of launch, you must slow the team down long enough to carefully consider the need for a custom organizational model and a rigorous learning process. Haste can be dangerous. The most expedient choice is usually to mimic the Performance Engine by transferring insiders to the Dedicated Team, by adopting existing titles and job descriptions, by utilizing existing planning templates, and so forth. You must help the team work through more thoughtful choices, reminding it that any errors in organizing and planning can create debilitating handicaps.

Then, you must make sure that the company accepts the right choices. The Performance Engine does not like to make exceptions. Heads of human resources do not like to offer unique job descriptions and compensation packages. Heads of IT would prefer if everyone followed the same processes and used the same systems. CFOs are often much happier if every unit reports performance on the same scorecard.

These desires for commonality are, of course, rooted in the Performance Engine's unquenchable thirst for efficiency. But efficiency should hardly be the guiding principle for an innovation initiative. The innovation leader should hope to be so lucky as to someday have the privilege of worrying first about efficiency. At launch, the uncertainties facing the typical innovation initiative (will revenues in year three be closer to $10 million or $100 million?) make the quest for efficiency of limited relevance.

Monitor Interactions with the Performance Engine

Even if an innovation initiative gets off to a good start, it will remain in conflict with the Performance Engine. The most common sources of conflict are resource constraints and fears that the initiative will somehow inflict damage on the Performance Engine—by cannibalizing a product or by damaging a brand, for example.

When conflicts arise, the Performance Engine almost always has the stronger bargaining position. It is bigger, it is more connected to powerful executives, and it usually has more immediate and more quantifiable arguments to support its needs. As a result, the innovation leader may struggle to get his needs prioritized.

That is unfortunate. After all, it makes little sense for a company to make a major formal commitment to an innovation endeavor from the top, only to undermine the commitment by withholding resources at a lower level in the organization. The short-term–long-term resource balance made at the senior levels should be aligned with the short-term–long-term resource balance made at day-to-day operational levels. As supervising executive, you must aid the innovation leader in the struggle for resources, striving for what is in the best interest of the company over the long term.

You must also help to ensure that there is a thriving partnership between the Dedicated Team and the Shared Staff. Because there are stark differences in how the two teams operate and how they are organized, they may not readily get along. A bit of intracompany rivalry is sometimes healthy and productive, but conflicts between the Dedicated Team and the Shared Staff can easily rise to the point where they inflict damage on the project. You must be watchful and help the innovation leader ensure that the tensions are maintained at healthy levels.

Stay Closely Engaged in a Rigorous Learning Process

Innovation leaders tend to disengage from the learning process because they believe that other tasks are more important. They are *always* in a hurry. We often hear innovation leaders talking in apocalyptic terms about what will happen, say, if they fail to get the new product out the door within six months. Sometimes these statements are legitimate, but disengaging from a rigorous learning process also has severe dangers.

Even an innovation leader who is diligent about following the mechanics of a rigorous learning process needs your help to ensure detached and unbiased interpretation of results. Tremendous pressure, high aspirations, and long hours mix to create an environment in which emotions can run high, higher still if the team has fallen behind plan. With such strains, the odds of drawing accurate lessons learned are low unless you help keep discussions as scientific and dispassionate as possible, grounded in evidence and data.

You should also be watchful of how your colleagues on the senior management team are shaping expectations for the initiative. If they begin touting the potential of the initiative too heavily, and especially if they start doing so to the press or to Wall Street analysts, the team will sense that falling short of plan is failing, and learning will come to a stop.

Shape the Endgame

Your final responsibility as supervising executive is to decide when the innovation initiative is over, for better or for worse.

For failing initiatives, it is unrealistic to expect that the innovation leader will call things to a halt. That is your responsibility. When you decide to move on, you have a few final tasks. First, you will want to consider whether the initiative produced anything that may be useful in future innovation initiatives. Second, you'll want to permanently document lessons learned from the initiative and make them available to future innovation teams.

Finally, and most importantly, you have to figure out what to do with the individuals on the Dedicated Team. If the consequences for those individuals are viewed as severe or unfairly negative, they will have an impact on future initiatives. Nobody will want to have anything to do with innovation. Remember, the team might have executed the initiative flawlessly only to have it fail anyway.

In the happier circumstance, a success, there is still work to do. Once an initiative has proved itself—that is, once its operations are routine and predictable—integrating the team more closely with the Performance

Engine may be appropriate. You may be able to achieve new efficiencies by combining Dedicated Team and Performance Engine processes. While you no longer need a rigorous learning process, the initiative's distinct performance scorecard probably *is* still needed. Be cautious. There are dangers in bringing the team too close to the established units, analogous to the dangers of going too far when integrating an acquired company.

Choose the Right Supervising Executive

After you have succeeded as a supervising executive, you might be asked: who can supervise the next major initiative? To do the job well, the supervising executive must be (1) powerful, (2) broadly experienced, and (3) in a position to serve the long-term interests of the company as a whole. Let's look at each of these criteria.

Powerful

In large corporations, power and status are generally commensurate with resources under command. But innovation initiatives start small. Therefore, at launch, innovation leaders tend to have very little power.

That can be a problem, because launch is when innovation leaders most need power in order to establish critical differences from the Performance Engine in organization and planning. They can get it only by drawing on the influence of the supervising executive, who must, in particular, be able to influence leaders of support functions such as human resources, IT, and finance.

Supervising executives must also be powerful enough to have access to sufficient resources to support the innovation initiative from launch to fruition. The fight to sustain funding can be tough. The Performance Engine never loses its enthusiasm for eliminating activities that do not contribute to short-term performance. Innovation initiatives are always at risk.

For the innovation initiative to have a realistic shot at sustaining the funding it needs, the supervising executive should be able to draw resources from a level in the organization that manages budgets that are at least one hundred times larger than the budget for the initiative. In practice, this means that the innovation leader should report at least one level higher up in the organization than the size of the budget for the initiative would otherwise suggest.

It would be a mistake, for example, for a leader of a $5 million innovation initiative to report to a leader of a related $50 million business unit. The problem is that the $50 million business unit almost certainly has much less than $5 million in cash to spare for innovation. It is probably expected to hit its profit target within a margin of a few hundred thousand dollars. Even if the business unit is able to take on the initiative at launch, it probably will not be able to sustain the commitment. Most innovation initiatives require *more* resources along the path to success.

Broadly Experienced

A hard-charging executive who has spent an entire career at one company, working her way up in the Performance Engine, may be an excellent candidate for *some* senior management roles. However, if she has only seen one organizational model and only managed proven lines of business, she is probably not well suited to supervising innovation.

One of the critical contributions the supervising executive must make is helping to shape and protect the team's custom organizational model. Executives who have seen many different kinds of organizations throughout their careers are likely to make better choices. Another critical contribution is in properly interpreting results. Experience managing new ventures or experience financing them, say, in the venture capital community, can be valuable in this role.

Able to Serve Company's Long-Term Interests

The supervising executive usually has multiple roles. If 90 percent of his job is to lead the Performance Engine—and especially if he feels that his performance review will almost entirely depend on how he does in his Performance Engine role—then that executive is too conflicted to do a solid job of supervising the innovation initiative. He will give too much weight to short-term performance and too little to long-term opportunity. Having innovation initiatives report to line executives in the Performance Engine is best avoided.

One alternative is to create a position for a chief innovation officer who supervises all major innovation initiatives through a separate budget. Another is for the innovation leader to report directly to the CEO or even to a board member. Or the innovation leader could report to an internal board of directors. The risk with a board, of course, is that when several people share responsibility, nothing gets done. But we believe that a board can be effective if each member of the board has clear and specific roles. For example, the chairperson could be responsible for evaluating the performance of the innovation leader and making decisions about continued funding. Another board member could be responsible for oversight of interactions with the Performance Engine. A third could advise the innovation leader on the organizational model for the Dedicated Team.

Oversee a Family of Related Initiatives

Let's imagine you have been promoted again, perhaps into a role with an increasingly popular title, chief innovation officer. You will be thinking about more than just one initiative. If your company has a clear and crisp strategic ambition, chances are that you will be pursuing families of innovation initiatives with similar characteristics. This gives you the opportunity for repeated innovation success.

Many of the stories we have shared in this book focus on just one of many initiatives that were all intended to push the company toward a larger objective. For example, at Dow Jones, the ambition of CEO Rich Zannino was to offer all of his customers, readers, and advertisers the best of both worlds—a single, cleverly integrated package of content across both print and online channels. To get there, he launched initiatives to overhaul each core business function, integrating print and online processes. (See examples in chapters 2 and 3.)

At Infosys, chairman Narayana Murthy's ambition was to assemble a complete range of information technology services for corporations so that clients could hold a single provider accountable for designing information systems, building them, and then running them. To achieve the objective, he launched a wide range of new services units, including Infosys Consulting. (See examples in chapters 3 and 4.)

At Thomson, Brian Hall's ambition was to serve law firms not just with tools for case law research but for all their information needs. To reach the goal, he launched two families of innovation initiatives. One was a set of new information products for litigators; the other, for law firm executives. (See examples in chapters 2 and 4.)

Crafting a clear innovation agenda that is logically tied to a powerful strategic intent has many benefits. First, funding for innovation initiatives is scarce. While scattering the available resources across a wide range of unrelated initiatives may yield some unexpected success stories, companies will generally only reach their highest aspirations when nearly all the innovation resources are aligned. Second, a clear innovation agenda focuses employees' innovation energies. Turning an employee base loose to pursue new ideas and new possibilities is usually more productive if the employees have a clear sense of what kinds of innovation are most valued. Finally, executing several related innovation initiatives is just easier. It allows companies to create families of innovation initiatives that reuse, rather than create from scratch, some aspects of organizational models and plans.

Some caution is due when pursuing this last benefit. We have emphasized the need for a custom approach to each initiative because every innovation initiative is a departure from the past, and each is in at least some ways unique; otherwise it wouldn't be innovative. Just as mimicking the Performance Engine can be deadly for an innovation initiative, so can mimicking another innovation initiative, if the two are too dissimilar.

So, how do you assess whether a set of initiatives can safely be grouped into a collective innovation family? Some basic guidelines are appropriate. Two initiatives can be grouped into the same family if they meet all of the following criteria:

- They are aligned with the same strategic objective.

- They are similar in form; for example, they are major process overhauls, new product launches, new service launches, or new business launches.

- They require Dedicated Teams with the same core functions and seek to leverage the same Performance Engine assets.

- They are of similar length (months, quarters, or years).

- They are of similar expense (hundreds of thousands, millions, tens of millions, and so on).

- They involve similar areas of uncertainty.

If a group of initiatives meets these criteria, then extending our principles from one initiative to many is fairly straightforward. It is simply a matter of applying common elements of the execution task at scale rather than reinventing the wheel each time. In table C-1, we have reframed the key topics in the book as questions that can be applied to an entire innovation family.

TABLE C-1

Moving from one initiative to many

Single innovation initiatives	An innovation family
Custom organizational model	***Custom organizational model***
What role can the Performance Engine take on in this innovation initiative? (chapter 1)	Can the Performance Engine take on the same role for *every* initiative in the family? (If not, they do not all belong in the same family.)
How will we staff the Dedicated Team? What insiders are needed? Are they available? (chapter 2)	What internally available skills are needed for this group of initiatives? As we transfer people to innovation projects, who will take their existing jobs?
Do we need to hire outsiders with new capabilities? What will it take to find and hire them? (chapter 2)	Do all the initiatives in this group require similar new skills? How will we build the new capabilities at the necessary scale? Do we need new recruiting pipelines? Training programs? M&A initiatives?
Does this initiative require that we create new and unfamiliar roles and responsibilities? (chapter 2)	Do we need to create new titles, job descriptions, and compensation plans that are common to all initiatives in the family?
Does the Performance Engine have the necessary slack time and slack resources to support the initiative? How will conflicts be resolved? (chapter 3)	How many initiatives can the Performance Engine support simultaneously? Which senior executive or senior management council will resolve resource conflicts?
What other tensions will arise between the Dedicated Team and the Performance Engine? Which senior executive can help create and sustain a productive relationship between the two? (chapter 3)	What specific tensions or conflicts affect *all* initiatives in this family? How can they best be managed?
Rigorous learning process	***Rigorous learning process***
What are the characteristics of the necessary planning process for this innovation initiative, so that assumptions are tested quickly and efficiently? (chapter 4)	Can all initiatives in the family share a common planning process or common planning templates? Can there be a single forum for evaluating the progress of all projects in this family?
What is the cause-and-effect hypothesis that we are testing? What are the critical unknowns? (chapter 5)	How are the cause-and-effect hypotheses for the initiatives in this family similar? Are some of the critical unknowns shared? Can they be tested just once for all initiatives?
What performance measures are relevant for the initiative? Are the metrics or the standards different from business as usual? (chapter 5)	What metrics do all initiatives in the family have in common? Can we modify our internal accounting systems to routinely present results for this family of innovation initiatives in a distinct format?
On what criteria should the leader be evaluated? What is the nature of the accountabilities? (chapter 6)	Can all leaders of initiatives within the family be evaluated on the same criteria? Can some productive internal competition between them be created?

(*continued*)

TABLE C-1 *(continued)*

How can we minimize the impact of emotion and bias when interpreting results? (chapter 6)	Are there common sources of bias that might affect all initiatives in the family? How can they be minimized?
Critical resources	*Critical resources*
Who is the right individual to lead this initiative?	Who are the leaders for this family? Do we have slack at this position? Do we need to hire to create slack?
To whom should the leader report?	Can the same executive or executive council evaluate *all* the initiatives in this family?
Do we have the capital needed not just to initiate this endeavor, but to follow through to fruition?	Given the company's capital budget, how many initiatives can the company pursue at one time, from initiation to fruition?

Help Shape a More Innovative Company

We have high expectations for you. We think that you will someday be promoted to CEO. When you do, the nature of your innovation challenge will change once again. You will have to influence innovation less directly and across a broader population of employees.

We think that one of the best ways to do so is to adopt a simple, teachable point of view about how innovation happens. We have seen that one powerful point of view is just a set of innovation truths that counter the most common innovation myths.

Unfortunately, myths about innovation run rampant in every industry. They have gained currency because there is tremendous hunger for insight into the challenge of making innovation happen but, until recently, little in the way of rigorous research. In any endeavor, when demand for new knowledge exceeds the ability of researchers to deliver it, conditions are ripe for the birth and proliferation of "solutions" that prove more popular than useful.

Here are the ten most common myths. If you become very sensitive to them and counter them at every opportunity, you will make a critical contribution to your company's environment for innovation.

Myth 1: Innovation Is All About Ideas

When one company we studied sought new ideas for expanding beyond its traditional product line, one of its early steps was to solicit ideas from its employees, particularly its sales force, which was closest to the customer. Through its extensive effort, the company generated over one thousand ideas, plus several hundred more from its product development organization.

Then, endeavoring to reduce the list, the company set up a series of special meetings and voting processes. The review of so many ideas was cumbersome, even overwhelming. Ultimately, the company decided it had the resources to move forward with only five of them.

The company's experience illustrates what we believe to be the most fundamental truth about innovation. While it is true that you can't even get started without an idea, the importance of the Big Idea Hunt is vastly overrated. That is why we have dedicated our research and this book to the other side of innovation, to *execution*. And you should encourage your company to shift more attention to the other side as well.

Myth 2: The Great Leader Never Fails

Where you find an overemphasis on great ideas, you often find an overemphasis on great leaders. Taken together, these two myths constitute what we think of as the romance of ideas and heroes. Even if you are unmoved by exaggerated tales of inspired underdogs overcoming long odds, you can be sure such stories resonate with many of the people inside your organization. These narratives usually are popular, but innovation is a real-world challenge, not a made-for-TV movie.

We do not dismiss the importance of choosing the right innovation leaders. However, choosing a talented leader is never enough. The inherent conflicts between innovation and ongoing operations are simply too fundamental and too powerful for one person to tackle alone.

Organizations are more powerful than individuals. Get the organizational choices right—build the right team with a custom organizational model for each innovation initiative—and a broad swath of managers, not just the great ones, can succeed as innovation leaders.

Myth 3: Effective Innovation Leaders Are Subversives Fighting the System

Popular innovation mythology has a lot to say about the best kind of innovation leader. They are risk takers, mavericks, and rebels.

The reality that innovation and ongoing operations are inevitably in conflict proves convenient for innovation myth makers. It provides the setting for rich drama. What does our hero do? Our hero engages in a noble battle with the pervasive and stubborn forces arrayed against innovation. Thus, we have the oft-heard innovator's mantra: break all of the rules.

You don't want to let this notion take hold in your organization. It leads nowhere. Innovation relies on a partnership between the Dedicated Team and the Performance Engine, and a break-all-of-the-rules attitude quickly undermines it.

We do not believe that innovation leadership is best thought of as civil disobedience. The odds are against mavericks. Moreover, an organization full of rebels fighting the system is not an innovation powerhouse; it is an undisciplined and chaotic mess.

Some of the popular ideas about innovation leaders are on target. Yes, they must be confident and determined, even unflappable. Yes, they must be unshakably optimistic. They must be able to motivate their teams to work toward a distant and uncertain vision. But great innovation leaders must also be humble. Only humble leaders recognize that their ideas are fallible, that they need help, and that the path to fruition is uncertain.

Myth 4: Everyone Can Be an Innovator

In the face of complexity, people want simple answers. It is not surprising, then, that the most widely shared model for making innovation happen is devastatingly simple: "Motivate and empower individuals at all levels of the organization to innovate." The model is also attractive because it affirms each employee's view of himself: "I am special." "I have something unique to offer." "I can innovate." "I can improve the world in front of me."

But the model overlooks a basic reality that all organizations face: resources are scarce, and the bulk of resources in any established organization must be dedicated not to innovation but to ongoing operations. Therefore, resources for innovation must be allocated carefully. By contrast, the turn-the-masses-loose approach spreads resources thinly and indiscriminately. It chops the available resources into tiny pieces—a few dollars here, a few there, a bit of free time here, a bit there—just so everyone can be involved.

Spreading resources in this fashion will result in three specific disappointments. First, it produces a disjointed overall effort. The sum of hundreds of individual aspirations is unlikely to aggregate to anything coherent. Second, it favors *very* small initiatives. Individuals pursuing their own inspirations with their limited free time can only execute tiny experiments. Finally, it overemphasizes the front end of the innovation process. One person can flesh out a big idea, but is unlikely to move it forward.

In part, the popularity of the turn-the-masses-loose approach is due to public perceptions that the model has made a few well-regarded companies particularly innovative. For example, 3M is famous for its practice of giving employees 15 percent of their time to pursue creative ideas of their own inspiration. Google is said to offer employees 20 percent of their time for the same purpose. These companies and others are no doubt delighted to cultivate reputations as happy homes for would-be innovators. But public perceptions are a vast simplification of what actually happens in these companies.

It is hard to see how such policies could possibly be affordable. Twenty percent of every employee's time is quite a bite into the P&L, especially just to generate some interesting ideas. Actually following up on even a fraction of the ideas would cost an even more outrageous sum, far beyond the slack resources available in any mature organization.

Despite these problems, we can't imagine a CEO saying, "Not everyone can be an innovator," and we don't recommend it. Every employee can *contribute* to innovation, but it is very important to communicate *how* he or she can contribute. Certainly, everyone can and should be involved in small experiments to improve performance in his or her direct sphere of responsibility. In addition, everyone can be an idea generator. Great ideas can come from anywhere. But to get beyond ideas, companies must concentrate their scarce resources for innovation—just a subset of employees, just a handful of ideas.

Myth 5: Innovation Happens Organically

Another common misperception is that innovation is by nature an organic, bottom-up process. Some executives are remarkably hesitant to direct innovation projects. Alas, beyond the smallest projects, little can bubble up.

Suppose a few employees with a common interest come together organically to discuss an interesting idea. Using whatever slack time they have available, perhaps lunch hours and late nights, such a team might actually start getting some work done.

But getting very far is difficult. Slack resources can be found only in tiny pieces throughout an organization. An organically formed team is unlikely to find a way to assemble a sufficient number of these tiny pieces to make anything significant happen. Adding to the difficulty, the little pieces of slack are not reliably available because of the fluctuating demands of ongoing operations. When day-to-day work becomes all consuming for one or more team members, even temporarily, organically formed innovation initiatives lose momentum or get tabled.

You don't want your company to pin its hopes entirely on an organic approach to innovation. The companies that do rarely produce anything more than small victories. They may initiate larger innovation projects, but they won't finish them. The only way to follow through is to make a formal and intentional resource commitment.

Myth 6: Innovation Can Be Embedded Inside an Established Organization

We are frequently asked, "How can I embed innovation in the very fabric of my organization?" The question is always asked in a way that suggests it must indeed be possible, so that innovation "just happens."

Some forms of innovation *can* be embedded. In the introduction, we discussed two possibilities. The *innovation = ideas + motivation* model is sufficient for continuous process improvement, and the *innovation = ideas + process* model works well for new product development, so long as each product is sufficiently similar to past products. But if you are at all interested in breaking out beyond the restrictive limitations of these two models, then you also need custom approaches for specific initiatives.

Beyond routine process and product innovation, embedded innovation is just implausible. That's because of the fundamental incompatibilities. The Performance Engine is inherently a hostile place for innovation. Trying to embed one inside the other will inflict severe damage on one or the other, or both.

Myth 7: Catalyzing Innovation Requires Wholesale Organizational Change

One executive we spoke with compared his company's experience trying to make innovation happen to "running face first into a concrete wall." He arrived at an important insight—that his organization was poorly designed for innovation. Exactly right! His organization, like all proven organizations, was designed for ongoing operations, not for innovation.

In exasperation, some managers overreact. They conclude that the problem is *everything* about the established organization. Their solution? Break the organization down and then build it back up so that it can innovate.

It sounds like a plausible approach and maybe even an inspiringly ambitious one, but you do *not* want this notion to gain any credibility in your company. Such an aggressive approach might make an organization much better at innovation, but at what cost? Such wholesale change will almost certainly diminish or even destroy the established business.

In reality, innovation does not require extensive change; it requires targeted change. In developing our recommendations in this book, we have held as our first obligation that we must do no harm to existing organizational capabilities. Innovation may divert resources from ongoing operations, it may even cannibalize the existing business over the long run, but it may not dismantle or damage the Performance Engine's organizational skills. Innovation *does* require substantial departures from organizational norms. However, these changes need affect only Dedicated Teams, not the entire organization.

For many CEOs and senior executives, this is good news. Many sense that they must choose either innovation or short-term performance. And, indeed, many of the intuitive actions that leaders want to take in favor of innovation seem only to come at a cost to the established business. But as we have shown, there is no need to choose. Companies can achieve simultaneous excellence in innovation and ongoing operations.

Myth 8: Innovation Can Happen Only in Skunk Works

Faced with the inescapable conflicts between innovation and ongoing operations, many companies believe that innovation requires a separate unit—a skunk works—that is completely isolated from the rest of the organization. Innovation leaders are often strong proponents of this idea. Because of ever-present conflict with the Performance Engine, there are many days when innovation leaders want to tell the rest of the organization to just go away.

But you don't want the innovators in your company to promote this mind-set. Beyond the idea stage, isolation rarely makes sense. Nearly every worthwhile innovation initiative is worthwhile in part because of the opportunity to leverage the company's existing assets and capabilities. In some cases, innovation leaders will want to leverage an existing sales force to get a new offering out the door. In other cases, they may want to manufacture a new product inside of an existing plant.

There are many possibilities, but in almost every case, leveraging an existing asset requires routine interactions with the established business. Therefore, there *must* be engagement between innovation and ongoing operations, between a Dedicated Team and the Performance Engine.

Myth 9: Innovation Is Unmanageable Chaos

How should innovation initiatives be managed? Some innovation leaders have a quick and ready answer: "Don't even try. Innovation is unpredictable. Therefore, it cannot possibly be managed."

The notion of innovation as chaos persists because of the widespread fascination with the Big Idea Hunt. Getting to that breakthrough insight, that brilliant idea, can be serendipitous and difficult to manage. But the remaining 99 percent of the innovation journey is entirely different.

Few companies recognize the sharp and jarring nature of the transition from ideas to execution—from the front end to the back end of the innovation process. So strident is the business community's obsession with the Big Idea Hunt that much of what you have heard, read, or think you know about innovation applies *only* to that hunt. Unfortunately, best practices for generating ideas have almost nothing to do with best practices for moving them forward. The other side of innovation is uncertain, but it is hardly unmanageable.

Iconic ice-cream maker Ben & Jerry's came to appreciate the stark difference between the front end and back end of the innovation process when it was acquired by Unilever. From its launch, Ben & Jerry's had embraced a fun, open, tolerant, and even irreverent environment, one that led to such enticing flavor names as Phish Food and Chubby Hubby. The CEO (that's chief *euphoria* officer, mind you) Walt Freese saw a connection between the culture and innovation: "The more fun people have, the freer they feel to come up with bold new ideas."

Naturally, when Unilever bought Ben & Jerry's, some saw the end of an era. They anticipated the consumer products giant would squash an innovative jewel. To the contrary, in Freese's view: "We have adopted a lot of process discipline and financial discipline from Unilever. We like the idea of a disciplined innovation process because it has helped us move forward with bigger, more complicated ideas."

Freese sees innovation as two different puzzles. When talking about ideas, he talks of irreverence. When talking about implementation, he talks of discipline. We agree.

Myth 10: Only Start-ups Can Innovate

Perhaps you, like many executives, have seen numerous innovation efforts struggle. If you have ever felt tempted to conclude that big companies should just throw in the towel and leave innovation to start-ups, you are not alone.

But the reality is that many innovation challenges are out of reach for start-ups. They can be tackled only by large and established corporations. (Table C-2 summarizes the innovation myths and innovation truths.)

We believe that large corporations have the most to offer in solving the biggest, most complex problems facing humanity—from global warming to the scarcity of clean water to the depletion of natural resources. Corporations have mammoth assets at their disposal, assets that entrepreneurial

TABLE C-2

Ten innovation myths

Myth	Truth
1. Innovation is all about ideas.	1. Ideas are only beginnings.
2. The great leader never fails at innovation.	2. When it comes to innovation, there is nothing simple about execution.
3. Effective innovation leaders are subversives fighting the system.	3. The primary virtue of an effective innovation leader is humility.
4. Everyone can be an innovator.	4. Ideation is everyone's job, as are small improvements in each employee's direct sphere of responsibility.
5. Innovation happens organically.	5. Innovation initiatives of any appreciable scale require a formal, intentional resource commitment.
6. Innovation can be embedded inside an established organization.	6. Innovation is incompatible with ongoing operations.
7. Catalyzing innovation requires wholesale organizational change.	7. Innovation requires only targeted change.
8. Innovation can only happen in skunk works.	8. Innovation cannot be isolated from ongoing operations. There must be engagement between the two.
9. Innovation is unmanageable chaos.	9. Innovation must be closely and carefully managed.
10. Only start-ups can innovate.	10. Many of the world's biggest problems can be solved only by large, established corporations.

firms can only dream of, from established brands to established networks of relationships to deep expertise in technology.

The CEOs whom we admire know this, and they are ambitious. Andy Grove, cofounder of Intel, in a letter published in *Portfolio* magazine in December 2007, encouraged two of these ambitious CEOs to set their ambitions higher still. He charged Lee Scott, CEO of Walmart, with revolutionizing health care by creating a new network of primary care clinics, and Jeff Immelt, CEO of GE, with building and commercializing an electric car.

We don't know if these are the specific ambitions that should top the innovation agendas for these companies, but we love the spirit of the letter. In particular, we admire the willingness of one of the most successful entrepreneurs in history to recognize that the world's most pressing challenges are beyond the reach of pure start-ups. We support Grove's call for CEOs to raise aspirations.

Some CEOs fear high aspirations. They are fated to mediocrity. Those that have the courage to aim high must renew their commitment to innovation. There is work to be done.

For more than a decade, innovation has been practically synonymous with the latest cool gadget. In the new era, innovation will not be about cool. It will be about profound change. It will not be about the NASDAQ; it will be about the *Fortune* 500. In the new era, the word *innovation* will convey breakthrough solutions for a peak world population of nearly 10 billion people, all striving for a better life, all facing the realities of a crowded and constrained planet.

Corporations face many pressures to act in a socially responsible manner. We'd like to apply a more powerful kind of pressure. We push for a day when CEOs are judged not just by profits, but also by the extent to which those profits resulted from innovations that contributed to solving the world's most pressing problems.

When you have a success story that you are proud of, please take the time to share it with us. We write about and speak about innovation. You have the power to make it happen, and we live vicariously through you. Please drop us an e-mail at vg@dartmouth.edu or chris.trimble@dartmouth.edu or interact with us at www.theothersideofinnovation.com, www.vijaygovindarajan.com, www.vg-tuck.com, or www.chris-trimble.com.

ASSESSMENT TOOLS

Assessment Tool 1

Objective: Determine how to divide the labor between the Dedicated Team and the Shared Staff. (See chapter 1.)

Step 1

Using table AT-1, list the skills required to execute the innovation initiative. Often it is helpful to start each skill description with an *-ing* verb. For example, *designing, engineering, manufacturing,* or *selling*. Then indicate whether or not the skill sets are available or not available within your organization. If you can hire outsiders with appreciably stronger skills (or, potentially, "hire" by acquiring a small company) and the improvement in skills might make a significant difference for the initiative, then mark not available.

In listing skills, be as granular as you need to be to differentiate skills that your organization has available from those it does not. For example, you may need to include both selling face to face and selling online if the initiative requires both skills and only one is available within your organization.

Part of the purpose here is to ensure that you think about *skills you need* before you think about *people you know* when building the Dedicated Team.

TABLE AT-1

	Skill	Available	Not available
A			
B			
C			

	Skill	Available	Not available
D			
E			
F			
G			

Every skill that you marked not available must be moved to the Dedicated Team.

Step 2

In this step, we consider *only* the skills that you marked available in table AT-1.

Let's imagine, for sake of discussion, that you marked skills C, E, and G as not available, and therefore you have moved them to the Dedicated Team. The purpose of this step is to determine whether any of the *remaining* skills—A, B, D, and F—also need to be moved to the Dedicated Team. They will need to be moved if the work relationships among A, B, D, and F in the Performance Engine are incompatible with what is needed for the innovation initiative. (Before proceeding, you may wish to review chapter 1.)

In table AT-2, create a list of each *pair* of skills for which there is a routine work relationship in the Performance Engine. If A and B routinely collaborate closely, or A routinely hands off work directly to B, there is a routine work relationship. You may find it helpful to draw a basic sketch of the work flow inside the Performance Engine. (See, for example, figure 1-1.)

TABLE AT-2

	Work relationships in the Performance Engine
1	A-B
2	B-D
3	D-F
4	

TABLE AT-3

	Work relationships needed for the innovation initiative
1	A-F
2	B-D
3	
4	

Note that a work relationship is about *getting work done*. (There are other types of relationships in business organizations—social, personal, mentoring, advisory, and so forth.) Also, work interactions that occur once in a while and on no predictable schedule are not routine.

Now, repeat the process for the innovation initiative, using table AT-3. Again, you need to consider only the skills that you marked available in table AT-1.

Next, identify any pairs that appear in table AT-3 but not in table AT-2. These are work relationships that are needed for the innovation initiative but do not exist in the Performance Engine.

One or both of the two skills in each of these pairs should be moved to the Dedicated Team. Otherwise, the pair is likely to struggle to coordinate schedules and get work done together without interfering with ongoing operations.

In our example, pair A-F appears in table AT-3 but not in table AT-2. Therefore skill A, skill F, or both A and F should be moved to the Dedicated Team.

Finally, in table AT-4, list any pairs that appear in *both* tables AT-2 and AT-3. In our example, only B-D appears in both tables AT-2 and AT-3.

Then, indicate whether each pair listed can have the *same* work relationship in both ongoing operations and the innovation initiative. Can the expectations that each party has of the other remain the same? In particular, do the power balance and operating rhythm remain the same?

If you answer no to any questions in a row in table AT-4, you must move at least one of the two skills in that pair to the Dedicated Team. Doing so allows a new relationship to develop, distinct from the relationship within the Performance Engine.

TABLE AT-4

	Pairs that appear in both tables AT-2 and AT-3	Same expectations?	Same power balance?	Same operating rhythm?
1	B-D	Y	Y	Y
2				
3				

Finally, any skill that has not been explicitly moved to the Dedicated Team through the previous steps may remain on the Shared Staff.

In our example, the work relationship between B and D is the same for both the innovation initiative and ongoing operations. Therefore B and D can remain on the Shared Staff, as can either A or F.

Assessment Tool 2

Objective: Qualitatively assess the risk of a Little Performance Engine problem. (See chapter 2.)

Step 1

Calculate the percentage of effective outsiders on the Dedicated Team.

TABLE AT-5

Source	Percentage	Adjustment	Effective outsiders
Inside the company	%	None	0%
Inside the company, but from a distinct and unrelated or only loosely related business unit	%	Divide by 2	%
Outside the company	%	None	%
Totals	100%	None	%

Step 2

Answer the following questions with a simple yes or no.

TABLE AT-6

Question	Yes	No
1. Have you explicitly defined or redefined the titles, roles, and responsibilities of everyone on the Dedicated Team?		
2. Have you insisted that every pair of individuals that had a routine work relationship in the Performance Engine has an explicit conversation about how its work relationship will be different as part of the Dedicated Team?		
3. Does the Dedicated Team have its own physical space so that face-to-face interactions are frequent and routine?		
4. Have you considered whether the skill set that has the greatest power in the Performance Engine should also be most powerful on the Dedicated Team and, if not, taken action to shift power?		
5. Have you created a custom set of performance measures for the innovation initiative?		
6. Does the team understand how performance measures will be interpreted and, specifically, how they will be interpreted differently from how they are viewed in the Performance Engine?		
7. Have you reconsidered any pay-for-performance incentives in the compensation packages of the Dedicated Team to be sure they are in line with the objectives of the innovation initiative?		
8. Have you made an explicit effort to create a distinct culture for the Dedicated Team that is in line with its		

Question	Yes	No
mission, activities, and objectives, especially as they differ from those of the Performance Engine?		
9. Have you resisted the natural impulse to duplicate Performance Engine processes?		
10. Have you resisted pressures from human resources, finance, or IT to conform to standard company policies in the name of fairness or efficiency?		

Step 3

Calculate your risk-avoidance points.

TABLE AT-7

Line	Instruction	Risk-avoidance points
1	Enter the percentage of effective outsiders from table AT-1. (Maximum number of points is 40.)	
2	Give yourself 4 points for every yes answer in table AT-2.	
3	Total. (Maximum number of points is 80.)	

Step 4

Interpret your score.

TABLE AT-8

< 40	Very high danger of a Little Performance Engine problem
40–55	Significant danger
55–70	Some danger
70 +	No danger

Assessment Tool 3

Objective: Identify actions that need to be taken to ensure a healthy partnership between the Dedicated Team and the Performance Engine. (See chapter 3.)

Step 1

Ensure that you coordinate formal resource allocations.

List all Performance Engine leaders who make formal and explicit resource allocations that affect your initiative. For example, the head of manufacturing may make explicit allocations of production capacity, choosing whether to manufacture Performance Engine products or a new product your innovation initiative is bringing to market.

TABLE AT-9

Performance Engine leader	Resource allocation decision
1.	1.
2.	2.
3.	3.

In addition, ensure that you have completed the following actions.

TABLE AT-10

Action	Check box
1. I have included all resource allocations made by Performance Engine leaders on the formally approved plan for the innovation initiative.	☐
2. I have discussed possible conflicts and contingency plans (e.g., sudden growth or sudden decline of the innovation initiative) with each Performance Engine leader *in advance*.	☐

Action	Check box
3. There is a clear appeals process to resolve conflicts, adjudicated by the supervising executive.	☐
4. I am paying for the explicit costs of what the Shared Staff provides (whether fully utilized or not) through an internal accounting transfer.	☐
5. Arrangements have been made to correct the Performance Engine leader's performance metrics so that they are isolated from the (potentially negative) impact of the innovation initiative.	☐

Step 2

Ensure that you have sufficient time and energy from the Shared Staff.

List groups of people (or functions) on the Shared Staff and note the times that they are under the greatest pressure to meet Performance Engine imperatives. For example, you might note that salespeople are under extreme pressure to close deals at the end of each quarter.

TABLE AT-11

Group or function	Busiest times

Does the Shared Staff have any of the following fears about the innovation initiative?

TABLE AT-12

Fear	Yes	No
1. It could cannibalize an existing product or service.		

Fear	Yes	No
2. It could make an existing process obsolete and put Performance Engine jobs at risk.		
3. It could reduce or put at risk incentive compensation.		
4. It might damage a brand.		
5. It might damage a customer relationship.		
6. It might damage any other Performance Engine asset.		
7. List any other possible fears:		

Next, ensure that you have completed the following actions.

TABLE AT-13

Action	Check box
1. I have engaged the supervising executive in actively promoting the importance of the innovation initiative to the Shared Staff, especially during their busiest times.	☐
2. I have considered ways to minimize the burden on the Shared Staff, especially during their busiest times.	☐
3. I have ensured that the supervising executive is aware of any specific fears of the Shared Staff.	☐
4. I am working with the supervising executive to persuade the Shared Staff that, despite their specific fears, the innovation initiative is in the long-term best interest of the company.	☐
5. I am paying for a reasonably approximated cost of the Shared Staff's time through an internal accounting transfer.	☐

Action	Check box
6. With the supervising executive, I have considered possible special targets or bonuses to motivate the Shared Staff to push the innovation initiative forward.	☐

Step 3

Avoid disharmony in the partnership.

Does (or might) the Shared Staff have any of the following resentments or unfavorable perceptions about the Dedicated Team? (If you are not sure, find out.)

TABLE AT-14

Perception	Yes	No
1. The Dedicated Team feels superior to the rest of the company.		
2. The Dedicated Team thinks that it is the most important group in the company.		
3. The Dedicated Team gets special treatment. It is not held to the same standards of performance as the rest of the company.		
4. The Dedicated Team is paid too well.		
5. The Dedicated Team can't be trusted.		
6. The Dedicated Team thinks it is or should be in charge of everything.		
7. List any other resentments or unfavorable perceptions.		

Ensure you take the following steps to reduce the likelihood of toxic tensions between the Dedicated Team and the Shared Staff.

TABLE AT-15

Action	Check box
1. I have worked with the supervising executive to directly discuss and mitigate the Shared Staff's resentments. The Shared Staff has a clear understanding of why the innovation initiative is in the company's long-term best interests, despite the short-term sacrifices.	☐
2. I closely monitor and eliminate any actions or behaviors of the Dedicated Team that may unnecessarily exacerbate any ill-will from the Shared Staff.	☐
3. I have made the division of responsibilities between the Dedicated Team and the Shared Staff very clear.	☐
4. I have strengthened common bonds by reinforcing the values and aspirations shared by both the Dedicated Team and the Shared Staff.	☐
5. Where possible, I have chosen insiders for the Dedicated Team roles that require the most intense interaction with the Shared Staff.	☐
6. I have tried to make it easy for the Dedicated Team and the Shared Staff to frequently interact face to face.	☐
7. I have worked with the supervising executive to modify the individual performance evaluations of the Shared Staff and Dedicated Team so that they explicitly call out each individual's ability to collaborate with the other group.	☐

Assessment Tool 4

Objective: Ensure you are following a process for disciplined experimentation. (See chapters 4 through 6.)

Prior to each business review, ensure you can answer yes to all of the following items.

TABLE AT-16

Action	Yes	No
1. There is a single, stand-alone plan for the innovation initiative.		
2. I am investing enough time in planning to learn as quickly as possible.		
3. I have not casually imported Performance Engine planning templates, budget categories, or performance metrics into the plan for the initiative. It is a custom plan.		
4. Using the tools in chapter 5, I have developed a clear action-outcome hypothesis of record about how the initiative will succeed.		
5. Everyone on the team understands and can clearly articulate our hypothesis of record.		
6. I have thought about how to resolve the most critical unknowns first so that we "spend a little, learn a lot."		
7. We are reviewing and revising the plan at least as frequently as we may be able to resolve a significant uncertainty or as often as we may need to make a significant change in direction.		
8. I have plotted all measures of performance as *trends*.		
9. Working with the supervising executive, I have made arrangements for the initiative to be reviewed in a separate forum from Performance Engine reviews.		
10. I have negotiated a clear framework for accountability with my supervising executive.		

Action	Yes	No
11. I understand that the predictions in my plan are probably wrong and that one of my critical priorities is making them better as quickly as possible.		
12. I am ready to review the common biases in interpreting results from an innovation initiative. (See last section in chapter 6.)		

SCHOLARLY FOUNDATIONS

We wrote this section primarily for academic scholars. In it, we show how we have been inspired by others, describe how streams of prior research have formed the foundation for our thinking, and draw connections between the principles advanced in this book and ideas advanced by others.

We wrote this book primarily for practitioners. The intent of our research, however, was also to advance new theory on the execution of innovation initiatives within established organizations. In doing so, we hope that we have opened doors for new research, including efforts to develop additional theory and endeavors to test the many hypotheses implied by our work.

Our Approach

Given our focus on the execution of innovation initiatives, we chose grounded theory building as our methodology—a qualitative, clinical, longitudinal, field-study–based approach. This was the appropriate choice because the theory in this area is only just emerging. It is best advanced by uncovering new concepts, not by testing hypotheses. Also, innovation execution is a dynamic and complex phenomenon. It requires intimate observation and necessitates consideration of data spanning several years, not just a snapshot.

We drew on several methodological guideposts, including:

Eisenhardt, Kathleen M. "Building Theories from Case Study Research." *Academy of Management Review* 14, no. 4 (1989): 532–550.

Eisenhardt, Kathleen M., and Melissa E. Graebner. "Theory Building from Cases: Opportunities and Challenges." *Academy of Management Journal* 50, no. 1 (2007): 25–32.

Glaser, Barney G., and Anselm L. Strauss. *The Discovery of Grounded Theory: Strategies for Qualitative Research.* New York: Aldine de Gruyter, 1967.

Yin, R. K. *Case Study Research: Design and Methodology.* Newbury Park, CA: Sage, 1994.

We immersed ourselves in researching, writing, analyzing, and comparing case histories of innovation initiatives. From each case study, we tried to understand: What is working? Why? Will this work for every company and every innovation initiative? What is proving difficult for the subject company? What is the root cause of the struggle? Will this struggle appear in every company and every innovation initiative?

These activities consumed the bulk of our time. That said, we also benefitted from a great deal of prior research.

Inspiration

Our work was inspired first and foremost by advances in the field of strategy. For many decades, strategists focused on how companies could protect competitive advantages. The 1990s, however, saw the rise of the opposite viewpoint—that playing defense is futile. The only companies that survive over the long run are those that innovate and create change.

Several strategists uncovered just how deeply the existing tools, analytical techniques, and mind-sets of strategy were tied to the objective of maintaining the status quo, and they challenged them. The works that had a strong influence on us include:

Christensen, Clayton M. *The Innovator's Dilemma.* Boston: Harvard Business School Press, 1997.

D'Aveni, Richard. *Hypercompetition.* New York: The Free Press, 1995.

Hamel, Gary. "Strategy as Revolution." *Harvard Business Review,* July–August 1996, 69–82.

Prahalad, C. K., and Gary Hamel. *Competing for the Future.* Boston: Harvard Business School Press, 1994.

One of us, Vijay, has particular interest and deep roots in global strategy. We drew further inspiration from:

Govindarajan, Vijay, and Anil Gupta. *The Quest for Global Dominance.* New York: Jossey Bass, 2001. See, especially, chapter 8, "Changing the Rules of the Global Game."

Prahalad, C. K., and Jan P. Oosterveld. "Transforming International Governance: The Challenge for Multinationals." *Sloan Management Review* 40, no. 3 (1999): 31–39.

The new strategic thinking, as groundbreaking as it was, left many questions unanswered. Most critically, even if companies could develop strategies focused on innovation and transformational change, could they execute them? This was the point of departure for our work.

Concurrent with our research, we've seen the rise of related new concepts and paradigms in strategy. The resource-based view identifies core capabilities—and the ability to extend them into new markets and opportunities—as a foundational source of competitive advantage. Dynamic capabilities—capabilities to create new capabilities—are also now recognized as foundational advantages. Skill in executing innovation initiatives is an illustration of a dynamic capability. See:

Eisenhardt, Kathleen M., and Jeffrey A. Martin. "Dynamic Capabilities: What Are They?" *Strategic Management Journal* 21, no. 10/11 (2000): 1105–1121.

Helfat, Connie, et al., *Dynamic Capabilities: Understanding Strategic Change in Organizations.* Malden, MA: Blackwell Publishing, 2007.

Peteraf, Margaret A. "The Cornerstones of Competitive Advantage: A Resource-Based View." *Strategic Management Journal* 14, no. 3 (1993): 179–191.

Teece, David J., Gary Pisano, and Amy Shuen. "Dynamic Capabilities and Strategic Management." *Strategic Management Journal* 18, no. 7 (1997): 509–533.

Wang, C. L., and P. K. Ahmed. "Dynamic Capabilities: A Review and Research Agenda." *International Journal of Management Reviews* 9, no. 1 (2007): 31–51.

Zahra, S. A., H. J. Sapienza, and P. Davidsson. "Entrepreneurship and Dynamic Capabilities: A Review, Model, and Research Agenda." *Journal of Management Studies* 43, no. 4 (2006): 917–955.

We also drew inspiration from the simple observation that it is through innovation that companies advance the interests of society at large most directly. See:

Govindarajan, Vijay, and Chris Trimble. "Not All Profits Are Equal." *Across the Board,* September 2002, 43–48.

The Big Idea Hunt

Our decision to focus on *execution* was reinforced by the tremendous volume of literature on the processes, tools, techniques, and organizational designs that lead to breakthrough ideas and creativity. To give just a few examples:

Drucker, Peter. "The Discipline of Innovation." *Harvard Business Review,* May–June 1985, 67–72.

Galbraith, Jay R. "Designing the Innovative Organization." *Organizational Dynamics* 10, no. 3 (1982): 5–25.

Hamel, Gary. "Bringing Silicon Valley Inside." *Harvard Business Review,* September–October 1999, 70–84.

Kelley, Thomas, and Jonathan Littman. *The Ten Faces of Innovation.* New York: Random House, 2005.

Kim, W. Chan, and Renée Mauborgne. *Blue Ocean Strategy.* Boston: Harvard Business School Press, 2005.

Because of the strength of these works and many more, we felt that we could achieve a much greater impact on practice by focusing on execution. One article that offers an interesting angle on why execution is more important than idea generation is:

Bhide, Amar. "Hustle as Strategy." *Harvard Business Review,* September–October 1986, 59–65.

Innovation Typologies

At the outset of our work, it seemed implausible to us that there could be a single recipe for innovation execution. We closely examined many authors' efforts to identify different categories of innovation initiatives. Works we found particularly useful include:

Abernathy, William J., and Kim B. Clark. "Innovation: Mapping the Winds of Creative Destruction." *Research Policy* 14, no. 1 (1985): 3–22.

Christensen, Clayton M. *The Innovator's Dilemma.* Boston: Harvard Business School Press, 1997.

Gatignon, Hubert, Michael L. Tushman, Wendy Smith, and Philip Anderson. "A Structural Approach to Assessing Innovation: Construct Development of Innovation Locus, Type, and Characteristics." *Management Science* 48, no. 9 (2002): 1103–1122.

Tushman, Michael L., and Philip Anderson. "Technological Discontinuities and Organizational Environments." *Administrative Science Quarterly* 31, no. 3 (1986): 439–465.

For the most part, these authors differentiate innovative ideas on the basis of their strategic impact. Most famously, Clayton Christensen differentiated disruptive ideas from sustaining ones. But there are many more categorizations. There are process, product, adjacency, and strategic innovations, for example. And there are radical, incremental, competence-enhancing, and competence-destroying innovations.

These typologies are powerful and useful for *developing* strategy. But were they equally useful for execution? Some researchers have made a few connections to execution challenges (for example, Christensen suggests that disruptive innovations require spin-offs), but we found these connections, in general, to be unsatisfying. They left many questions unanswered.

We suspected that the best typology for *execution* would come from the inside out, not from the outside in. It would be rooted in the inner workings of organizations at a granular level, not in comparisons between the intended market impact of an innovation initiative and a business unit's existing competitive strategy.

We imagined that we would develop numerous recommendations in an *if–then* form. That is, *if* your innovation has the following operational characteristics and *if* your organization has the following operational capabilities, *then* you need to follow these steps.

In the end, we saw that no new typology was needed. This was certainly the hardest-won realization of our project. A critical step was eliminating from consideration the forms of innovation that well-managed organizations are already quite good at— continuous process improvement following the *innovation = ideas + motivation* model and routine product development following the *innovation = ideas + process* model, as described in the introduction.

Once we did this, we saw that the general was far more powerful than the specific. Our most important recommendations could be applied broadly. They worked for new processes, new products, and new businesses. They worked for disruptive and sustaining innovations. They worked for competence-enhancing and competence-destroying innovations. And they worked for incremental or radical innovations. We think this is an important contribution to the body of theory on innovation.

Corporate Entrepreneurship

The stream of research focused on corporate innovation and corporate entrepreneurship is the body of work most directly related to our own. The literature stretches back several decades. Useful starting points for investigation include:

Leifer, Richard, Christopher M. McDermott, Gina Colarelli O'Connor, and Lois S. Peters. *Radical Innovation: How Mature Companies Can Outsmart Upstarts.* Boston: Harvard Business School Press, 2000.

Macmillan, Ian, and Rita McGrath. *The Entrepreneurial Mindset: Strategies for Continuously Creating Opportunity in an Age of Uncertainty.* Boston: Harvard Business School Press, 2000.

McGrath, R. G., T. Keil, and T. Tukiainen. "Extracting Value from Corporate Venturing." *MIT Sloan Management Review* 48, no. 1 (2006): 50–56.

Pinchot, Gifford. *Intrapreneuring: Why You Don't Have to Leave the Corporation to Become an Entrepreneur.* New York: HarperCollins, 1985.

Entrepreneurship is an extremely broad field, almost as broad as business itself. We felt that we could best build on this literature by narrowing our focus. We studied only execution. And, we did not consider challenges that entrepreneurs face in either a new venture context or a corporate context. We only focused on execution challenges that innovation leaders face precisely because they are inside corporations.

The most important of these challenges, we believe, is derived directly from the fundamental incompatibilities between innovation and ongoing operations. Corporations maximize profitability by making every task, activity, and process as repeatable and predictable as possible. Innovation, however, is by nature exactly the opposite—nonroutine and uncertain.

General Barriers to Innovation

While the corporate entrepreneurship literature is optimistic and directive in tone, many of the other research streams that we drew on highlighted barriers to innovation.

Much of the literature in this category highlights why corporations may struggle just to take the first step—to commit to an innovation initiative. They may not, for example: (1) if it cannibalizes the existing business, (2) if current customers are not clamoring for the innovation, (3) if executives are instinctively oriented to reducing risk and variability, (4) if executives become complacent after years of success, or (5) if executives seek to retain power by remaining focused on their areas of greatest competence. For more, see:

Ahuja, Gautam, and Curba M. Lampert. "Entrepreneurship in the Large Corporation: A Longitudinal Study of How Established Firms Create Breakthrough Innovations." *Strategic Management Journal* 22, no. 6/7 (2001): 521–543.

Benner, Mary, and Michael L. Tushman. "Exploitation, Exploration, and Process Management: The Productivity Dilemma Revisited." *Academy of Management Review* 28, no. 2 (2003): 238–256.

Chandy, Rajesh K., and Gerard J. Tellis. "Organizing for Radical Product Innovation: The Overlooked Role of Willingness to Cannibalize." *Journal of Marketing Research* 37, no. 4 (November 1998): 474–487.

Christensen, Clayton, and Joseph L. Bower. "Customer Power, Strategic Investment, and the Failure of Leading Firms." *Strategic Management Journal* 17, no. 3 (1996): 197–218.

Ghemawat, Pankaj. "Market Incumbency and Technological Inertia." *Marketing Science* 10, no. 2 (1991): 161–171.

Hannan, Michael T., and John Freeman. "Structural Inertia and Organizational Change." *American Sociological Review* 49, no. 2 (April 1984): 149–164.

Hill, Charles W. L., and Frank T. Rothaermel. "The Performance of Incumbent Firms in the Face of Radical Technological Innovation." *Academy of Management Review* 28, no. 2 (2003): 257–274.

Pfeffer, Jeffrey. *Power in Organizations.* Marshfield, MA: Pitman, 1981.

Stuart, Toby E., and Joel M. Podolny. "Local Search and the Evolution of Technological Capabilities." *Strategic Management Journal* 17 (1996): 21–38.

Tripsas, Mary, and Giovanni Gavetti. "Capabilities, Cognition and Inertia: Evidence from Digital Imaging." *Strategic Management Journal* 21, no. 10/11 (2000): 1147–1161.

Utterback, James M. *Mastering the Dynamics of Innovation.* Boston: Harvard Business School Press, 1994.

Although we studied what happens *after* a commitment to an initiative is made, these works were useful. The same forms of resistance that prevent innovation initiatives from being launched in the first place also tend to hinder initiatives once they are under way.

We were most influenced by these sources in chapter 3, in which we identified specific tensions between the Dedicated Team and the Performance Engine and recommended steps for mitigating them. As the sources listed focused on problems, we have tried to build on them by elaborating on the solutions.

Organizational Design

The core prescription in this book is that every innovation initiative requires a team with a custom organizational model and a plan that is revised only through a rigorous learning process.

In developing the specifics for the first part of the prescription—a team with a custom organizational model—we have drawn on works that spell out the fundamentals of organizational design, including:

Galbraith, Jay. *Designing Organizations.* San Francisco: Jossey-Bass, 2002.

Thompson, James D. *Organizations in Action: Social Science Bases of Administrative Theory.* New Brunswick, NJ: Transaction Publishers, 1967 and 2003.

There is also a rich stream of research that connects elements of organizational design to broad constructs such as responsiveness, adaptability, flexibility, and innovativeness. See, for example:

Graetz, F., and A. C. T. Smith. "The Role of Dualities in Arbitrating Continuity and Change in Forms of Organizing." *International Journal of Management Reviews* 10, no. 3 (2008): 265–280.

Guttel, W. H., and S. W. Konlechner. "Dynamic Capabilities and Competence Obsolescence: Empirical Data from Research-Intensive Firms." Proceedings of the International Conference on Organizational Learning, Knowledge, and Capabilities, June 14–17, 2007, Richard Ivey School of Business, Spencer Conference Centre, London, ON, Canada.

Harreld, J. B., C. A. O'Reilly, and M. L. Tushman. "Dynamic Capabilities at IBM: Driving Strategy into Action." *California Management Review* 49, no. 4 (2007): 21–43.

Jansen, J. P. P., G. George, F. A. J. Van den Bosch, and H. W. Volberda. "Senior Team Attributes and Organizational Ambidexterity: The Moderating Role of Transformational Leadership." *Journal of Management Studies* 45, no. 5 (2008): 982–1007.

Plowman, D. A., L. Baker, T. Beck, S. Solansky, M. Kulkarni, and D. V. Travis. "Radical Change, Accidentally: The Emergence and Amplification of Small Change." *Academy of Management Journal* 50, no. 3 (2007): 515–543.

Raisch, S., and J. Birkinshaw. "Organizational Ambidexterity: Antecedents, Outcomes and Moderators." *Journal of Management* 34, no. 3 (2008): 375–409.

Salomo, S., and H. G. Gemunden. "Research on Corporate Radical Innovation Systems." *Journal of Engineering and Technology Management* 24, no. 1–2 (2007): 1–10.

Sine, W. D., H. Mitsuhashi, and D. A. Kirsch. "Revisiting Burns and Stalker: Formal Structure and New Venture Performance in Emerging Economic Sectors." *Academy of Management Journal* 49, no. 1 (2006): 121–132.

Smith, W. K., and M. L. Tushman. "Managing Strategic Contradictions: A Top Management Model for Managing Innovation Streams." *Organization Science* 16, no. 5 (2005): 522–536.

Tushman, M. L., and C. A. O'Reilly. "Ambidextrous Organizations: Managing Evolutionary and Revolutionary Change." *California Management Review* 38, no. 4 (1996): 8–30.

Yadav, M. S., J. C. Prabhu, and R. K. Chandy. "Managing the Future: CEO Attention and Innovation Outcomes." *Journal of Marketing* 71, no. 4 (October 2007): 84–101.

Our prescription calls for a special new subunit, the Dedicated Team, that is both differentiated from and integrated with the existing organization. The themes of differentiation and integration have a long history in the general literature on organizations.

Lawrence, Paul R., and Jay William Lorsch. *Organization and Environment: Managing Differentiation and Integration.* Boston: Harvard Business School Press, 1967.

Dougherty, D. "Reimagining the Differentiation and Integration of Work for Sustained Product Innovation." *Organization Science* 12, no. 5 (2001): 612–631.

Innovation is a differentiation-integration challenge at its most extreme. The differences between the Dedicated Team and the Performance Engine must be night and day. Yet, there must be a thriving partnership between the two. The degree of difficulty is underappreciated by many practitioners.

The challenge of building the right kind of organizational model can be broken down into two parts: (1) creating the distinct subunit, and (2) linking it to the existing organization. For additional insight into why the former is both critical and complex, see:

Cohen, Wesley M., and Daniel A. Levinthal. "Absorptive Capacity: A New Perspective on Learning and Innovation." *Administrative Science Quarterly* 35, no. 1 (1990): 128–152.

Eisenhardt, Kathleen M., and Behnam N. Tabrizi. "Accelerating Adaptive Processes: Product Innovation in the Global Computer Industry." *Administrative Science Quarterly* 40, no. 1 (1995): 84–110.

Ghemawat, Pankaj, and Joan E. Ricart i Costa. "The Organizational Tension Between Static and Dynamic Efficiency." *Strategic Management Journal* 14 (1993): 59–73.

Govindarajan, Vijay, and Praveen Kopalle. "How Incumbents Can Introduce Radical and Disruptive Innovations: Theoretical and Empirical Analyses." *Journal of Product Innovation Management* (forthcoming).

Leonard-Barton, Dorothy. "Core Capabilities and Core Rigidities: A Paradox in Managing New Product Development." *Strategic Management Journal* (special issue, Summer 1992): 111–125.

More often than not, practitioners recognize the need for differentiation without appreciating the opposing need for integration. Several authors have described why both are important, as well as the complexities of making the partnership work:

Day, Jonathan D., et al. "The Innovative Organization: Why New Ventures Need More Than a Room of Their Own." *McKinsey Quarterly* 21, no. 2 (2001): 20–31.

Dougherty, Deborah, and Cynthia Hardy. "Sustained Product Innovation in Large, Mature Organizations: Overcoming Innovation-to-Organization Problems." *Academy of Management Journal* 39, no. 5 (1996): 1120–1153.

Iansiti, Marco, F. Warren McFarlan, and George Westerman. "Leveraging the Incumbent's Advantage." *MIT Sloan Management Review* 44, no. 4 (2003): 58–64.

Katila, Ritta, and Gautam Ahuja. "Something Old, Something New: A Longitudinal Study of Search Behavior and New Product Introduction." *Academy of Management Journal* 45, no. 6 (2002): 1183–1194.

Markides, Constantinos, and Constantinos D. Charitou. "Competing with Dual Business Models: A Contingency Approach." *Academy of Management Executive* 18, no. 3 (2004): 20–31.

Teece, David J., "Profiting from Technological Innovation: Implications for Integration, Collaboration, Licensing, and Public Policy." *Research Policy* 15, no. 6 (1986): 285–305.

Tushman, Michael, and Charles O'Reilly. "The Ambidextrous Organization." *Harvard Business Review*, April 2004, 74–81.

The corporations we studied offered many additional insights into the various tensions that arise between innovation and ongoing operations and the many creative ways to overcome them.

It is one thing to recognize that an innovation initiative needs a differentiated-yet-integrated organizational form—that is, a partnership between a Dedicated Team and the Performance Engine. It is quite another to define the roles of each entity.

Indeed, we observed some well-run innovation initiatives in which the Dedicated Team was tiny and limited to a small but important activity and others in which the Dedicated Team did almost all of the work. One of the particularly challenging questions that we knew we had to address for readers was how to know what balance of responsibilities was appropriate. This was our focus in chapter 1.

We drew critical insight from studies that differentiated new product development efforts that established product development organizations *could* and *could not* tackle.

Clark, Kim B., and Steven C. Wheelwright. "Organizing and Leading 'Heavyweight' Development Teams." *California Management Review* 34, no. 3 (1992): 9–28.

Henderson, Rebecca M., and Kim B. Clark. "Architectural Innovation: The Reconfiguration of Existing Product Technologies and the Failure of Established Firms." *Administrative Science Quarterly* 35, no. 1 (1990): 9–30.

These authors focused on the importance of *work relationships* in establishing the limits of a product development team's capabilities. We have tried to build on their work by exploring the specifics that define work relationships—their depth, power balance, and rhythm.

Also, we have seen that their critical insight extends beyond product development to work relationships within any function and even work relationships that cross functions. As long as *any* two people maintain routine Performance Engine responsibilities, their work relationship will be nearly impossible to change. This significant constraint on what the Performance Engine can do is often overlooked.

Planning and Learning

In developing the second half of our prescription—a plan that is revised only through a rigorous learning process—we have benefited from a great depth of literature on organizational learning. Much of this research elaborates on why it is so hard for organizations to learn from experience. For example, see:

Hedberg, Bo L. T., "How Organizations Learn and Unlearn." In *Handbook of Organizational Design*, edited by Paul C. Nystrom and William H. Starbuck. Oxford: Oxford University Press, 1981.

Levinthal, Daniel A., and James G. March. "The Myopia of Learning." *Strategic Management Journal* 14, Special Issue: Organizations, Decision Making, and Strategy (Winter 1993): 95–112.

Levitt, Barbara, and James G. March. "Organizational Learning." *Annual Review of Sociology* 14, no. 1 (1988): 319–340.

March, James G., Lee S. Sproull, and Michal Tamuz. "Learning from Samples of One or Fewer." *Organization Science* 2, no. 1 (1991): 1–13.

Our discussion of the biases inherent in the learning process (chapter 6) is consistent with these articles.

However, our intent was to focus on solutions, not problems. Any solution must start with a structured and disciplined learning process, one that is grounded in the scientific method, and one that tests an explicit action-outcome hypothesis. Sounds reasonable enough, but past research has shown just how challenging it is just to get that far.

Executing the scientific method is hard, even for scientists. And, businesspeople are generally much less familiar with it. Businesspeople have succeeded only in turning formal experimentation into routine practice in certain limited contexts. Furthermore, corporate planning systems just get in the way. They were designed for ongoing operations, not for experimentation. For more, see:

Brews, Peter J., and Michelle R. Hunt. "Learning to Plan and Planning to Learn: Resolving the Planning School/Learning School Debate." *Strategic Management Journal* 20, no. 10 (1999): 889–913.

Delmar, Frederic, and Scott Shane. "Does Business Planning Facilitate the Development of New Ventures?" *Strategic Management Journal* 24, no. 12 (2003): 1165–1185.

Duncan, Robert, and Andrew Weiss. "Organizational Learning: Implications for Organizational Design." *Research in Organizational Behavior* 1 (1979): 75–123.

Huber, George P. "Organizational Learning: The Contributing Processes and the Literatures." *Organization Science* 2, no. 1 (February 1999): 88–115.

Levinthal, Daniel, and James G. March. "A Model of Adaptive Organizational Search." *Journal of Economic Behavior and Organization* 2, no. 4 (1981): 307–333.

Spear, Steven, and H. Kent Brown. "Decoding the DNA of the Toyota Production System." *Harvard Business Review,* September–October 1999, 97–106.

Wilson, Edward O. "Life Is a Narrative." In *The Best American Science and Nature Writing 2001,* edited by Edward O. Wilson and Burkhard Bilger. Boston: Houghton-Mifflin, 2001.

Nonetheless, we are optimistic. These articles simply point to the need for corporations to follow two very different sets of planning practices—one for ongoing operations and one for innovation.

Another extensively documented barrier to learning is the tendency to remain committed to targets even after new evidence suggests that the targets were unrealistic. Several factors create this tendency, but the most powerful is the well-known instinct to evaluate a manager's performance based first and foremost on whether or not the manager hits his or her targets.

That works well in the Performance Engine. But in innovation initiatives, targets are guesses. Overcommitment to targets undermines learning. Furthermore, demanding that innovation leaders hit targets erodes the psychological safety that is necessary for risk taking in the first place. For more, see:

Cyert, Richard M., and James G. March. *A Behavioral Theory of the Firm.* Englewood Cliffs, NJ: Prentice Hall, 1963.

Edmondson, Amy. "Psychological Safety and Learning Behavior in Work Teams." *Administrative Science Quarterly* 44, no. 2 (1999): 350–383.

Grant, Robert M. "Strategic Planning in a Turbulent Environment: Evidence from the Oil Majors." *Strategic Management Journal* 24, no. 6 (2003): 491–517.

Lant, Theresa K., and Amy E. Hurley. "A Contingency Model of Response to Performance Feedback." *Group & Organization Management* 24, no. 4 (1999): 421–437.

Lant, Theresa K., and Stephen J. Mezias. "An Organizational Learning Model of Convergence and Reorientation." *Organization Science* 3, no. 1 (1992): 47–71.

Lounamaa, Pertti H., and James G. March. "Adaptive Coordination of a Learning Team." *Organization Science* 33, no. 1 (1987): 107–123.

Maciariello, Joseph A., and Calvin J. Kirby. *Management Control Systems: Using Adaptive Systems to Attain Control.* New York: Pearson Education, 1994.

McGrath, Rita G. "Exploratory Learning, Innovative Capacity, and Managerial Oversight." *Academy of Management Journal* 44, no. 1 (2001): 116–131.

Merchant, Kenneth A. *Rewarding Results: Motivating Profit Center Managers.* Boston: Harvard Business School Press, 1989.

Staw, Barry M. "The Escalation of Commitment to a Course of Action." *Academy of Management Review* 6, no. 4 (1981): 577–587.

Ouchi, William. "A Conceptual Framework for the Design of Organizational Control Mechanisms." *Management Science* 25, no. 9 (1979): 833–848.

Practitioners need to maintain discipline in the Performance Engine. They also need a distinct framework for accountability for innovation leaders, one that is flexible enough to be applied to a wide range of initiatives. This was our emphasis in chapters 4 through 6.

Some of the specific principles in chapter 4 build directly on others' ideas. See, for example:

Gersick, Connie J. G. "Pacing Strategic Change: The Case of a New Venture." *Academy of Management Journal* 37, no. 1 (1994): 9–45.

March, James G., and Johan P. Olson. "Organizational Learning and the Ambiguity of the Past." In *Ambiguity and Choice in Organizations,* edited by James G. March and Johan P. Olson. Bergen, Norway: Universitetsforlaget, 1976.

Other authors have also noted the trade-off between a systematic approach to learning and first-mover advantage:

Boulding, William, and Markus Christen. "First-Mover Disadvantage." *Harvard Business Review,* October 2001, 20–21.

Lieberman, Marvin B., and David B. Montgomery. "First Mover (Dis)advantages: Retrospective and Link with the Resource-Based View." *Strategic Management Journal* 19, no. 12 (1998): 1111–1125.

Makadok, Richard. "Can First-Mover and Early-Mover Advantages Be Sustained in an Industry with Low Barriers to Entry/Imitation?" *Strategic Management Journal* 19, no. 7 (1998): 683–686.

Particularly in chapter 5, our recommendations emphasize the importance of having good conversations about cause-and-effect hypotheses. This is consistent with:

Barringer, Bruce R., and Allen C. Bluedorn. "The Relationship Between Corporate Entrepreneurship and Strategic Management." *Strategic Management Journal* 20, no. 5 (1999): 421–444.

Other authors have focused on measurement, quantification, and analysis. See, for example:

Anthony, Scott. *The Silver Lining.* Boston: Harvard Business Press, 2009.

Kaplan, Robert S., and David P. Norton. *The Balanced Scorecard*. Boston: Harvard Business School Press, 1996.

McGrath, Rita G., and Ian C. MacMillan. "Discovery Driven Planning." *Harvard Business Review*, July–August 1995, 44–54.

Our view is that as innovation initiatives evolve and uncertainty is reduced, the emphasis should gradually shift from qualitative conversations to quantitative analysis.

INDEX

ACKNOWLEDGMENTS

We could not have completed this book without a great deal of assistance from many talented people.

First, none of our work would have been possible without the funding we received through the William F. Achtmeyer Center for Global Leadership at Tuck. We are grateful to Bill Achtmeyer, both for his generosity and his personal friendship. Also at Tuck, we thank Dean Paul Danos for his strong support; Bill Little, a research partner whose energy opened doors for several interviews that proved critical to our overall effort; and Beth Perkins, without whose administrative support we'd both be hopelessly lost.

We received a wealth of inspired editorial input throughout the production of this book, from early concepts to the final comma. In particular, we thank our agents, Todd Shuster and Esmond Harmsworth; our editors at Harvard Business Review Press, Jacque Murphy, Kathleen Carr, Kirsten Sandberg, Allison Peter, and Jane Gebhart; and two editorial professionals who have supported us for many years, Anita Warren and Lorraine Anderson.

We are indebted to all of the executives who offered their valuable time for interviews with us. We acknowledge, in particular, those who opened doors for us at the six corporations that were most crucial to our effort: Jerry Fishman at Analog Devices, H. J. Markley at Deere & Company, N. R. Narayana Murthy at Infosys, David Hanssens at Thomson-Reuters, Matt Goldberg at Dow Jones, and David Yuan at IBM.

Finally, we are grateful, once again, to all of the people who helped us with our first book, *Ten Rules for Strategic Innovators—From Idea to Execution,* which lay an important foundation for this book.

ABOUT THE AUTHORS

VIJAY GOVINDARAJAN (known as V. G.) and CHRIS TRIMBLE are on the faculty at the Tuck School of Business at Dartmouth. They have dedicated the past ten years to studying a single challenge, one that vexes even the best-managed corporations: how to execute an innovation initiative.

In 2005, they published the international bestseller *Ten Rules for Strategic Innovators—From Idea to Execution*. The *Wall Street Journal* published a Top Ten Recommended Reading list that placed *Ten Rules* alongside well-known titles including *Freakonomics, The Tipping Point*, and *Blink*. *Strategy & Business* magazine recognized *Ten Rules* as the best strategy book of the year.

V. G. and Chris have published together in the *Harvard Business Review*, the *MIT Sloan Management Review*, the *California Management Review*, *BusinessWeek, Fast Company*, and the *Financial Times*. Their article "Organizational DNA for Strategic Innovation" won the Accenture Award for the best article of the year in the *California Management Review*.

Most recently, V. G. and Chris worked with Jeff Immelt, chairman and CEO of General Electric, to write "How GE Is Disrupting Itself," the *Harvard Business Review* article that introduced the notion of *reverse innovation*— any innovation that is adopted *first* in the developing world.

V. G. is the Earl C. Daum 1924 Professor of International Business and the founding director of Tuck's Center for Global Leadership. He was the first professor in residence and chief innovation consultant at General Electric.

V. G. has been named as: Outstanding Faculty (*BusinessWeek*, in its "Guide to the Best B-Schools"), Top Ten Business School Professor in Corporate Executive Education (*BusinessWeek*), "Superstar" Management Thinker from India (*BusinessWeek*), Top Five Most Respected Executive Coach on Strategy (*Forbes*), Top 25 Management Thinker (*The London Times*), and Outstanding Teacher of the Year (MBA students).

V. G. has worked directly with 25 percent of the *Fortune* 500 corporations including Boeing, Coca-Cola, Colgate, Deere, FedEx, Hewlett-Packard, IBM, J.P. Morgan Chase, Johnson & Johnson, New York Times, Procter & Gamble, Sony, and Walmart. He is a regular keynote speaker in CEO forums and major conferences including the World Innovation Forum and BusinessWeek CEO Forum.

V. G. received his doctorate and his MBA, with distinction, from the Harvard Business School.

He posts regular blogs for *Harvard Business Review* (www.hbr.org) and *BusinessWeek* (www.businessweek.com), and at www.vijaygovindarajan.com.

CHRIS's career mixes rigorous academic research with hard-nosed practical experience. His interest in innovation within large organizations developed early in his career, when he was a submarine officer in the U.S. Navy.

Chris has worked with dozens of top corporations, spending much of his time working directly with innovation leaders. He is a frequent speaker on the topic of innovation and has spoken all over the world.

Chris holds an MBA degree with distinction from the Tuck School and a bachelor of science degree with highest distinction from the University of Virginia.